Tide
Changes

A True West Coast Fishing Adventure

by
Dave Holland

Webb Publishing
Kelowna, BC, Canada

Editors: Helen Duggan, Jill Veitch
Illustrations: Loraine Kemp
Cover photo: The *Antique*, shortly after I bought her in 1975. I was out, *proudly* getting the feel of the boat. Special thanks to Vicky Hurford for thoughtfully taking this photo from the end of the Lund gas float. Little did I know then where it might wind up.

ISBN: 978-1-927056-08-0   All rights reserved.
Tide Changes: A True West Coast Fishing Adventure.
Copyright by the author © 2014 Dave Holland. Parksville, British Columbia, Canada.

Printed and bound in British Columbia, Canada. 2014

Library and Archives Canada Cataloguing in Publication

Holland, Dave, 1951-, author
    Tide changes : a true West Coast fishing adventure / by Dave Holland.

ISBN 978-1-927056-08-0 (pbk.)

    1. Holland, Dave, 1951-. 2. Fishers--British Columbia--Sunshine Coast--Biography. 3. Salmon fisheries--British Columbia--Sunshine Coast. 4. Sunshine Coast (B.C.)--Biography. I. Title.

SH20.H65A3 2014   639.2092   C2014-907330-5

Dedication

In memory of my good friend
Christopher Paul Taylor
Thanks for the unforgettable times we had together.

Contents

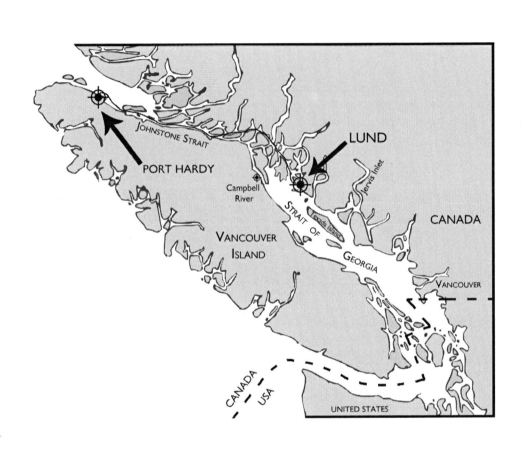

Foreword

Many times over the years I have been asked the question, "How did a guy from Hamilton Ontario become a fisherman on the west coast of British Columbia?" In my usual way, I would try to sum it up as best I could, but really I'm not sure I ever completely explained the journey; there is so much more to it than just a simple and short response.

When I reflect back at that time in my life, I realize that there is definitely a story here worth sharing. Not being a writer by trade I experienced many long gaps when I did not pick up the pen, but every now and then I would get the urge to continue, and twelve years later, it is done.

Amazingly enough, the feelings I had and the memories of that time have never waned. To this day so much is crystal clear and I guess that in itself says a lot. Originally I wanted to share my youth with my children and family but eventually, as I moved forward, I wanted to also *thank* so many people who were, way back when, such a positive influence in my life.

The title *Tide Changes*, I think, seems to best represent what one can go through when pursuing their dreams. We all have experienced the highs and lows, the ebbs and flows in life. Often one dream can lead to another, or maybe change, but seldom do they ever completely go away. Perhaps there's some serenity in that thought.

When I discovered more about myself at an early age, I set

out to try and make my dream a reality. So, with a mixture of hard work, lots of determination and of course that little thing all of us can use now and then, "luck", I started on my way. When combined with youth, inexperience and, at times, just plain not knowing any better, I now had the recipe for an *adventure*. And it certainly was.

Everything in this story actually happened and, having looked back at certain particular events, I feel somewhat thankful that I am here to share them with you. The names are the same and to those whom I've mentioned in this story, I have certainly tried to portray you in the most respectful of manners, for the benefit of both you and your families. It was, however, never hard to accomplish that here; there have been so many special people. To those whom I have not mentioned, my apologies. You hold a spot in my memory if not on paper.

That period of time can still tug at my emotions, for even now, after going over this story again and again, a smile comes to my face in some places and a tear appears just as easily in others. I am so grateful to have experienced that kind of passion in my life.

Enjoy!

Port Dover lighthouse.

Early Years

There is a sound that regularly signals the start of a new day. It can be loud or soft, and it can take on many different forms, but its greeting is a constant. On one particular morning in July 1964 my father gently started my day when he nudged my shoulder and said, "It's time to get up and go fishing." It was very early, 3:00 o'clock to be exact; I slowly dressed then walked quietly to the kitchen table. My family and I were on vacation in Port Dover, Ontario, a quaint little town located on the south eastern shore of Lake Erie. We had come here for many summers, usually two to three weeks at a time when my father had his annual holidays. As always we rented a cabin at Terrace View Cottages; a beautiful place owned by Al and Dorothy Blake with whom, to this day, I have remained very close. I have never forgotten Al's strong handshake and Dot's warm hug every year we visited.

Often Dad would take his three kids—me, my brother Craig and my sister, Denise—fishing down to the pier, on which a large red and white lighthouse welcomed boats in and out of the narrow harbour. Standing on the large cement structure that surrounded the lighthouse we would lower our lines into the water. We'd run a small weight that touched bottom first, followed by a big fat dew worm on a hook above it, then wait anxiously for a nibble in hopes of catching a perch, carp or whitefish. They were just some of the species common to the lake. Occasionally we caught something; a foot-long perch was always the best for eating.

We looked out onto the water or back toward the boardwalk where the arcades and music played loudly. The smell of food permeated the air courtesy of the best foot long hot dogs and fries anywhere. Several rides, including a small roller coaster and go carts, were close to the beach and pier where we stood. Port Dover was a great place; an escape from the humdrum of city life. None of this, however, not the rides, the music or food smells caught my attention on this particular morning. Mr. Blake had managed to talk one of the local commercial fishermen into taking me out for the day to see how fishing was really done. Despite not feeling well the previous day I really wanted to go. Dad made sure I had a big breakfast, to carry me over, in case it would be a while before the next meal. After a large bowl of cereal and four pieces of toast, he drove me down to the dock where I climbed aboard a commercial fishing vessel named *M.W.*

Much of what happened next is rather vague. I remember the smell of the dock and water in the air as the boat left the shelter of the harbour in the early morning darkness. At about 10 minutes into the journey, we passed the lighthouse and headed towards Long Point, where the nets would be set for the morning. It was going to be about a 3-hour run. The 45-foot boat started to slowly rock back and forth as we headed further out into open water.

It was not going to be a calm day. The wind was gusting, and after about an hour of rolling around, I started to feel sick. I asked the captain if I could lay down somewhere and I climbed into one of the upper berths next to the exhaust pipe that ran up from the engine room below. It provided additional warmth to that area of the boat. The combination of warm air and the tossing of the boat lulled me into a state of drowsiness; it was not a good feeling. The next thing I knew, I had deposited my breakfast all over the bunk. In my delirium, I reached up with my hand, only to grab the hot exhaust pipe, and burned it; the morning was quickly deteriorating.

At this time the owner turned the boat around and started heading back to port. I felt bad as it seemed I had ruined their day's fishing. Once tied up, I remember apologizing to him, and he graciously acknowledged that it was too rough to fish that day anyway.

My first brush with boats and water was not a good one; at the young age of 13, the unfortunate experience stayed with me for a while, but I soon moved on. Little did I know then where this moment in time might lead me in the years to come.

From an early age, and for whatever reason, I seemed to have a strong connection with the outdoors. I grew up in Hamilton, Ontario, which is also known as Steeltown, and that it was. Dad worked at Dofasco (Dominion Foundries and Steel Company) and raised us on his income. He liked his job and I remember him telling me that it was important to enjoy what you did. "Whatever you choose to do, son, strive to be the best at it," he told me and I have always tried to live up to those words. My father's side of the family was Scotch-Welsh and my mother's side was Polish-Ukrainian; it made for a healthy mix. We were, as they say, true Canadians, and your typical middle class family of the day. Dofasco was a good employer; Dad worked there for 37 years. Mom stayed home with the three of us kids, looking after many of the demands needed to raise a family. My younger brother, sister and I were lucky, we had great parents. I remember clearly missing out on another opportunity later in the same year as that first fishing experience; Mom asked me one day if I would like to go with her to Toronto and see a band play in a concert. I said no thanks. I felt it might interfere with some of my sports activities at the time and besides music, then, was not on my priority list. So Mom boarded a bus in Hamilton herself and travelled to Maple Leaf Gardens to see The Beatles. She had a great time and to this day I still think that was pretty cool on her part.

I went to high school at Southmont Secondary from Grades 9 to 13. I was an average student; for me, school was OK but I was not really sure what I wanted to do or what I wanted to be. I played football, although I was not a starter and played sparingly. Much of the time I kept the bench warm, but that was OK. I worked hard to make that team, lifting weights after classes at either the school or at a friend's house. I really developed my strength that year, those were fun times and I loved sports. Whatever I may have lacked in skills I made up for with "heart". I had lots of it. I played hockey in the Dofasco Minor Hockey League until I was 15. I then tried out for the high school hockey team at 16 and was disappointingly the last cut. There were many good players trying to make the squad during those years. That team went on to big things and in the years 1969 and 1970 came second in all of Ontario. It was my almost-claim-to-fame. Oh well!

That same year dad helped get me a summer job at the steel mill, but come September, I was back at school; grade 13.

This is such a delicate time in life; so many thoughts and decisions can surround us in our teen years. I had a friend, Bob who sat in front of me in math class. While the teacher was talking, I would be drawing pictures of wildlife, wolves, eagles and other things. I would show these to Bob and he'd laugh. "Maybe you should be a wildlife artist," he would tell me. I felt drawn to the outdoors. Something was gnawing at me then but I did not know what it was.

With so much going on around me, I was not able to graduate that year. At 17, I did not want to return to a summer job at Dofasco so, along with 25 other guys my age, I signed on to a Junior Forest Ranger Program. We wound up in a place called Schreiber, Ontario, at the very top of Lake Superior. If it was outdoor work I was wanting, this was it. It was our job to supply two campgrounds with firewood and maintain them. The pay wasn't great, we got $4.00 a day, but room and board were supplied. All in all it was a great summer. I made friends with some of the other guys and we stayed in touch for years afterward.

That fall I did not have the urge to go back to high school and redo my grade 13. I thought maybe of enrolling at a college in North Bay, Ontario to take their forestry course; having grade 12 allowed me to apply for entrance there. I remember driving to the college in Dad's car to check it out in September that year. For whatever reason, I decided after arriving that this program was not for me and I headed back to Hamilton. Really, I did not know what I wanted to do or be at this stage of my life.

Not working or attempting to finish my education was not an option in our home. So I decided that I would satisfy my urge to see more of the outdoors and all it could offer. At seventeen, in October of 1969, I said goodbye to my family, boarded a train in Toronto and headed west to British Columbia.

On the three day train ride west I had a lot of time to think. I wondered what to expect on the other side of Canada and where I might find some work. I was interested in becoming a logger, having some experience at that from my summer's work, little though it was. Where I was going I knew no one at all and had no connections. However I was not short on two things: ambition and stubbornness. Whatever I was looking for, I was determined to find it.

Upon arriving at the train station in Vancouver, the first thing I needed was a place to stay for the night. With only my knapsack holding all my worldly possessions in hand, I started walking down the main street from the train terminal. That first night I stayed at a YMCA close by; it was cheap and offered a room of my own. Next morning I set about finding work and a more permanent place to stay. I picked up the Vancouver Sun classifieds and answered the ad for a boarding house located at West 23rd and Oak Streets. It was $100 per month, room and board.

My basement room offered a small bed and dresser for clothes. There were 5 other people in the house and all had their own rooms. There were 2 students attending UBC and 3 elderly men. We usually shared supper every night at a large table in the dining room. Dinner was served up by the woman in charge, who went by the nickname Mommsy, and was both landlady and cook. She was a Hungarian woman who spoke English fairly well. At times, though, I struggled to understand her but she always managed to get her message across by either raising her voice or pointing. When Mommsy talked, you listened! She would often be found in the small kitchen peeling potatoes or stirring a steaming stove-top stew with a roll-your-own-cigarette hanging from the side of her mouth. Such moments, I recall, were not good times to bother her. So all of us would stay out of her way and sit patiently at the table until dinner was ready. We were a diverse group of individuals coming from many walks of life. I would ask questions, hoping to learn as much as I could. I remember George in particular, one of the students. He was especially knowledgeable about the logging end of things and was very helpful in directing me to the right place to look for a job. I did not have a lot of money and would have to find work very soon.

Within a few days, and again through the paper, I answered an ad and landed a job cleaning apartments on a city block in Vancouver. The hours were long and did not offer a lot of pay but it would be enough to cover my room and board with some left over. Regularly, when I had time, I would keep checking in at the forestry offices in town. However, I had two things against me: I had no direct experience and it was the wrong time of year. During the cold months, logging slowed down or would stop altogether depending on how severe the weather was. Few companies, it seemed, were hiring and my timing was certainly unfortunate. However none of this dampened my spirits; I had lots to keep me busy.

Fall passed and then winter. I remember that my first Christmas away from home was a hard one; I missed my family. It was great having freedom and to be on my own but, like many others my age, I came to realize and appreciate what I'd had. I often wrote letters home just to feel connected with my family.

By April of the following year, I had managed to set aside some money thanks to the job and of course my modest existence. I longed to see more of the west coast. Vancouver was a nice city but it was still a city and I wanted to see more of the mountains and trees that so far had only been in the distance. With some of the finances I had managed to save I decided to buy a racing bike: a good, affordable and cheap source of transportation.

The bike was a 10-speed Peugeot and at the time, that particular model rivalled Gitane for top position in the bike manufacturing world. It cost me $110 but it was worth it to have my own freedom and method of transportation as the bus, by now, had become a little repetitious.

In May I planned to head up the Sunshine Coast and then over to Vancouver Island. Shortly after finalizing the details of the trip I left my job. I said my farewells at the boarding house and set out on what was to be a two-month adventure. It was the start of a journey that would effectively change my life immensely and form a strong connection to the west coast that would always lure me back.

According to plan, I travelled north from Vancouver and stayed at campgrounds as far up as Saltery Bay. I returned to the city after one week then continued by ferry from Vancouver to Swartz Bay in Victoria. Somewhere along those travels I had purchased a book called *Adventure with Eagles,* written by Dave and Lynn Hancock. I was fascinated with wildlife from an early age, birds especially, and now I had an opportunity to maybe see them up close. The Hancocks had a small wildlife reserve in Saanichton and I decided that their place would be my first stopover on the island. I arrived in the afternoon and introduced myself to them. Their place was a refuge for orphaned or injured animals. They showed me around a bit before we entered a smaller separate building where, inside, was a fairly large caged enclosure that housed three one year old cougars. They were orphaned at a very young age and brought here as kittens. Their hackles were up and they were spitting and clawing at the cage. That was a memorable moment for me.

And then I watched from a distance as Lynn entered the cage to feed them. She was the only one that could approach them at close range and even from where I was standing it was very intimidating.

All this wildlife made for quite a place to visit. I do remember seeing an injured Bald Eagle up close; it was a very memorable afternoon. Reluctantly, I left too soon, but I needed a place to camp for the night. During our short visit I had expressed an interest in carrying camera gear for the opportunity to work beside wild life photographers in remote areas and they gave me the names of a few people I could contact in Victoria. I thanked them and set off.

I decided to bypass Victoria at this time and headed for Brentwood Bay. This was a quicker route for me. A small ferry would leave regularly, navigating across Saanich Inlet to Mill Bay, on the western shore of the inlet. This short but picturesque ride across the water would save the dozens of miles required to circle the full length of the deep inlet by land. I spent the night in Bamberton Provincial Park.

It was a great trip, just me and my bike; total freedom. I gradually worked my way up island to Parksville, which was as far north as I would travel on this journey, and stayed a while at Rathtrevor Beach, my soon-to-become favorite campground at the time. From Parksville I cycled along the road that led to Port Alberni and eventually I passed through the majestic landscape of Cathedral Grove. The trees here are all first growth; they were huge. I remember stopping by a stream in the grove and having a cool drink of mountain fresh water. *Not many places where you could do that*, I thought. That creek water was cold and crystal clear but so refreshing. I continued the long climb to the top of Mount Arrowsmith but then decided to forgo the ride into Port and instead, turned the bike around on top of the "hump" and then glided back down the steep hill. It was a quick trip to the bottom, I remember, almost too fast. I had to ease on the brakes every so often so as to not get out of control.

At this point of the journey I headed south to Victoria where I spent several days and nights. I slept in Beacon Hill Park, where I found the top row of the baseball stands to be a safe and quiet place to sleep.

Really, the whole time I spent travelling the island that summer was an amazing time for me. I loved what I had seen of the place and dreamed that one day this might become my home.

By summer's end, however, I was feeling homesick and decided to return to Hamilton. I had seen almost every campsite one could in my travels along this part of the west coast. I was in good shape, but longed for my mother's home cooked meals; I could only survive for so long on fruit, bread and every camper's staple, or at least mine, Brunswick sardines! At 19 cents a can they were affordable, tasty and even came with their own self-contained opener.

Once back in Ontario I decided to try one more year of Grade 13 but at a different school, Sir Wilfred Laurier. Mom and Dad took me back in at home and I did what I could to graduate. I played a little more football that year but again I fell short with the grades. I discovered that I really did not have much interest in school anymore; it was to be my last attempt at academics.

The freedom of living on my own a year earlier had made me more independent and after school was over I moved out and shared a house with seven other guys. My roommates were all students attending McMaster University; rent for me was $25 per month in a big, old brick house on Locke Street. I landed a job at Westinghouse Canada where they made appliances. The plant was a short bus trip away from home but when the weather was good, I often rode my now much-travelled bike back and forth to work.

I was paid $4.00/hour with 8 to 4 and 4 to 12 shifts, Monday through Friday. The money would be enough for me to live on. Some of the students boarding at the house enjoyed listening to my stories of the west coast. One, in particular, Peter Elliott, also had the urge to "go west", so we made plans to leave after school was out in mid-May. He had a 10-speed bike much like mine. My urge to go back to the west coast had never left, and I looked forward to this next trip.

We arrived at the Vancouver train station early in June and with our belongings strapped to our backs, we headed for the closest ferry to Victoria. We never really had a planned destination in mind so we just took it a day at a time, staying at provincial parks each night and starting again fairly early in the morning. I had my dream of logging and Pete thought he would like to try working in a mine; Campbell River was to be our parting place. He continued north to Port Hardy and eventually landed a job at Utah Mines.

Meanwhile I stayed in Campbell River. The first night there on my own, I decided to sleep under the stars at the closest beach I could find. There was a quiet spot north of the local ferry terminal where I rolled out my sleeping bag and being tired, quickly fell into a slumber. At about 2:00 am I awoke to the feeling of cold water lapping at my feet. It was to be my first physical experience with the rising tides of the ocean. I embarrassingly slid everything up to where I assumed the ground would be safe and dry and eventually fell back into a deep sleep.

The next night found me at the Quinsom Campground and within a few days I landed a job as a tree planter. It was there that I met my good friend, Chris Taylor. I did not think to pack a lunch that first day of work, but Chris offered me half of his rations. It would, without knowing it then, be the start of a friendship that lasted for many years. Planting trees was good work for me. I loved being outdoors and enjoyed the daily routine, working five days with weekends off. A truck would pick us up in front of the campground every morning then take us to a designated area in the mountains where we would start planting. Wherever we were it was the same; working our way up or down a side hill.

Like so many things, there's a process in tree planting and a learning curve involved. First I dug a small hole with the mattock they provided, a hand tool much like a pick-axe. Then from a bag full of trees strapped to my shoulder, I would insert a small 8-inch seedling in the ground and cover the area back up with dirt. I would press firmly around the plant with my hands or foot to be sure the seedling was secure and in place. This done, I then moved a couple of steps over to allow for adequate spacing and start again. A person could cover a lot of ground in a day. The truck we arrived in carried extra trees and when your bag was empty, you restocked and kept on going. By four in the afternoon, though, you were ready to board the truck and head home. It was enough for one day.

We looked forward to weekends off and in the warmer months frequently headed for the beach. It was on one of those visits, on a particularly hot Saturday in late June, that I would have another brush with Mother Nature; this time it was a little more serious than an advancing tide.

Chris and I had met two girls at the campground who were travelling through Vancouver Island. They were from Ireland so Chris, being from the area, decided to show them some of the local scenery. We decided on a hike along an established trail that would lead us to a place called Seymour Narrows. It was not long before we emerged from the wooded area and found ourselves on a flat low-lying piece of land with the sea at our footsteps. This beautiful shoreline location was known as Race Point. For those not familiar with coastal waterways, a narrows is a small channel through which larger open areas of water are forced into by the tides. There are several spots along the Vancouver Island coastline but Seymour Narrows is the largest one, siphoning the broader waters on the north and south side of the geological feature through a passage between Vancouver Island and Quadra Island. Race Point is located pretty much at the narrowest part of this stretch of water and the resulting effects from this natural phenomenon are very strong tides that can run up to 12 knots depending on the stage of tidal change. I of course knew nothing about this at the time.

It was a hot summer day and after this lengthy hike I was hot. On the spur of the moment and without saying a word, I quickly removed my t-shirt and jumped in to cool off. The water was frigid on impact and in the split second it took me to resurface, I did not see Chris or the girls I may have been trying to impress. I looked to my right and they were standing, open-mouthed, about 20 feet upstream from me and seemed to be rapidly moving away. Fear gripped my body as I reached for a piece of bull kelp that was in front of me. Fortunately it had attached itself securely enough to the rocks and managed somehow to hold my weight even under the strong pull of the tide. I clung to this small natural lifeline and ever so slowly, it seemed, the current drew me towards shore. Chris reached down, grabbed my arm and dragged me back onto dry land. "What are you doing?" he yelled. Feeling drained, I said nothing; clearly I had no idea. The current did not appear to be running very hard and luckily for me, at the time it probably wasn't. Regardless, I felt the power and force of it. I lay still for a long time, not saying a word, feeling the warmth of the sun on my body yet shivering at what had just happened. In time I would find many places where a person can enjoy a swim in the Pacific Ocean but Seymour Narrows is not one of them.

A few days later I came home from work only to find someone had cut the lock and chain and taken my bike; a big loss for me. So many great memories now gone, as we had covered a lot of ground together by then. It was upsetting. Chris was renting a cabin south of Campbell River and offered me a place to stay. I remember that being a great option as camping life was starting to wear a little thin on me, especially now that I had no way of getting around. I was quite relieved to find myself in a house with a few luxuries where it was also warm and dry.

Logging

My tree planting days came to an end when after much persistence I finally landed a job as choker man for Elk River Timber. The break I needed! They had a camp based nine miles south of Gold River; I would be making $8.25 per hour. For the time, that was pretty good money. I would stay in camp five days a week and spend the weekends in Campbell River.

My first day was one I will not forget. It was a hot day in early July and I was wearing the usual loggers' clothing: hard hat, heavy jeans, a grey Stanfield wool sweater and gloves; the only bare spots were my face and neck. The bugs were horrendous. I was bitten so badly that blood was running down my neck. When returning to camp at day's end I could not eat; I felt nauseous and I went to my bunk to lie down. It got better the next day, as I seemed to have developed some immunity and also regained my appetite.

There was no reason to go hungry in camp. The food was unbelievable. You worked hard and ate like a horse; I sure had an appetite then. After a typical steak dinner, which included as much as you could eat with all the trimmings, I still took one or two extra steaks back to the bunkhouse to munch on later. Breakfast was eggs, any way you wanted, cereal, toast, fruit, bacon, sausages, whatever. You would make your own lunch from a separate table then board the waiting truck that took you to your work site for the day. For all this food, the charge was $2.50 a day and was deducted from your paycheck. It was no wonder a lot of operations closer to small towns eventually started to commute daily. The days of camps were coming to an end in some areas; they had become too expensive to run. Logging camps still exist in remote parts of the coast, but within a year after I left Elk River, they closed our camp down and the loggers commuted every day from Campbell River. For the workers with families it was a lot better to be home every night.

Logging can be dangerous work and requires concentration at all times. I moved up to the position of rigging slinger fairly quickly. This meant I was in charge of signaling to the yarder operator when to stop the chokers near the logs and then, once connected, I'd signal him to pull ahead and drag the logs up the side hill to the landing area. This was done using an electronic device attached to my belt that triggered a loud horn located at the landing site. One beep meant stop and three beeps meant to go ahead. I was in charge of the choker man, making sure the logs were securely strapped with the cables. Then once we were safely clear and out of the bite, I'd signal to take them away. A thick one and a half inch cable was connected to the yarder and from there to two large stumps at the bottom of the hill, forming a triangle. The chokers were attached to the bull shackles on the mainline side of the set up and they would be dragged uphill or downhill by the yarder. The other side of the line was called the "haul back." Heavy steel straps with "eyes" were also wrapped around two notched stumps at the base of the side hill and they supported large 80-pound steel blocks through which the main cable from the yarder ran. The hook tender was in charge of our side of the operation and he would notch the next appropriate stump so when all the logs were removed from beneath that length of the mainline, the lines would be swapped over. We would then start again at the top of the next row and work our way back down, repeating the process.

In late fall of that year we were on a particularly steep side hill. There was a sprinkling of snow on the ground but not enough to cover anything. Our hook tender, on cold days when it looked like we would be closer to the bottom of the site, would start a fire so we were warm during lunch time. It happened frequently, as it seemed more often than not, we were in that position; eating only in the landing area when we were close to the top. The chaser's job was generally to look after the landing site and disconnect the chokers from the logs when they were in place. Once this was done, the yarder operator sent everything back down to us and we'd start the process all over again. When it was time to eat, the chaser would also put our lunches in a gunnysack, tie them to the rigging and send them to us. I would blow the whistle to signal stop at the base of the stump and our half hour lunch break would begin.

For whatever reason, on this day my lunch was not in the sack and I was hungry. In the meantime when I'd blown to stop the rigging to retrieve our food, the yarder shut down his machine after he had put the usual tension on the haul back line and slackened the main. Impatiently I blew the whistle to take the empty sack back up hoping someone would get the message. The choker man and hook tender were over by the fire and I was standing behind the line, twenty feet to the side of one stump. The yarder, I learned later, on my signal went back to the machine, fired it up and started to bring the main line in without taking the tension off the haul back side. I heard the hook tender yell "Get Down!" as the cable snapped about 100 feet to my left. Like a big black snake it recoiled from all this tension and slid by over top of where I lay flat to the ground. Everything was still for a moment and they ran over to make sure I was alright. It was way too close of a call.

I remember being shaken but after taking a moment to check myself over, another emotion came to me: anger. I put my hard hat back on and step-by-step started the long trek up the hill to the landing. I forget exactly what I said when I reached the top but I know it was something I would not want to repeat in this story. I showed the chaser where my lunch was, behind one of the tires of the yarder, where I would usually put it. I then turned and walked back down the hill. It never happened again.

However dangerous the work could be I was happy working there and enjoyed the lifestyle that came with it. Being in camp for five days seemed to give a person a little more reason to live it up when he got to town and I was no exception. I would usually rent a motel room for the weekends and, being my generous self, I'd buy my share of beer at the local pub. I would eat in restaurants so it did not take long to chew through my pay check. Logging work seemed to revolve around this kind of lifestyle especially if you were young and single. You worked hard and played hard.

Yes, the life of a logger. Some nights out on the town we would run out of money and Chris, being his enterprising self, found a way to get us through to last call: arm wrestling. It was a pretty big thing at the time and it would not be uncommon to see this kind of activity going on around you. Like all, I started out as the challenger. Being in good shape then I soon found out I really had the right build and arm for it. The bet, quite often, was the loser had to buy a beer for the winner. I never lost, so in those days in the bar, Chris and I never ran out of beer. I faced guys bigger and stronger looking than me but I still came out on top. Of course both opponents had to set up properly but the trick, I found, was when someone said "go" my adrenalin rush kicked in immediately and I went at it hard, never backing off until my opponent's arm gradually hit the table. I was good for maybe three to four challenges at a time before a little soreness would come in and it was time to rest. My left arm was never quite as good as my right but it wasn't until many years later that I eventually met my match. It was certainly fun while it lasted.

When the snow got too deep, logging became dangerous and it would be time to close down for the winter. I remember the day this happened that first year. The choker man and I were clearing snow away from a log so we could find a place to wrap the cable around it. Once the chokers were in place we cleared out of the way; only then would I signal the engineer to go ahead on the turn. When things get buried under snow it's hard to tell if you're totally clear of all danger. Some branches below our feet started to move and we had to hightail it back further out of the way. Our woods foreman saw this and decided to close it down. Safety had to come first, as even during ideal conditions it could be dangerous work. But winter passed quickly and we were soon back at the job come the following spring. I stayed with Elk River Timber through to late June 1972, two years almost to the day. It had been an exceptionally dry and hot period of time then and there was an early summer shutdown that year. When the bush became tinder dry, any logging activity could be a potential fire hazard.

Around that time, I was missing home somewhat and again had the urge to go back to Hamilton. I decided to leave my job and told the woods foreman of my plans. I thanked him for the opportunity to work there. It was a great experience for me and I left Elk River Timber with a good report and a few more stories to tell others. Before leaving for Ontario, though, I had an experience that, when looking back, was one of those moments that probably steered my life in a whole new direction.

I met two brothers in Campbell River, Rob and Chris Kelly. They owned a little fish boat called *The Comet* which was tied up at the main Campbell River government float. We were at a party together one night and talked about going fishing in the morning. We stayed up fairly late, despite having to get up at 4:30 to catch the "morning bite". I stayed on the boat, sitting in the wheelhouse's only seat, while Rob and Chris slept down below. I was excited at the prospect of fishing and had no trouble staying up the rest of the night. I woke them up just before first light and they slowly got things organized to start the day. They fired up the motor, slipped the lines free from the dock and off we went, heading in the direction of Cape Mudge. By that point I was pretty tired so I decided to catch up on a little sleep of my own.

I woke up two hours later to a banging sound and looked up to see a 5-pound salmon sail into their small fish box on deck. I quickly got up from down below, not wanting to miss a thing.

There in their checkers, the landing area for fish, lay about 40-45 beautiful, silver Coho salmon; some were still moving about. Rob and Chris worked the lines methodically up and down, snapping flashers and spoons off and on, until everything was back in the water. How it all worked seemed a bit of a mystery to me then; I watched and said little, taking it all in.

Every twenty minutes or so they would repeat the procedure removing what fish were there, then putting everything back down where the flashers would spin slowly as we moved through the water, trying to entice more fish to bite. Around 11:00 o'clock we headed back into Campbell River to sell the fish. There were about 55 Coho for the morning's effort. We pulled up to the cash buyer, where the cleaned fish were weighed and a slip was made up with all the details. Rob and Chris were then paid $250! *That's not bad for a mornings work*, I thought. I did not know it at the time but I was hooked. I made my way back to Vancouver and a few days later boarded the train back east to Toronto with memories of that day's fishing still fresh in my mind.

Hamilton had not changed much but it was sure good to see family and friends again. Things were pretty much booming there, as they were all across the country; work was plentiful. Soon after arriving home, I acquired a job, again at Westinghouse Canada. Mom and Dad took me back in one more time, and charged me a little for room and board. My living at home again was an adjustment for everyone after being on my own for two years, but I enjoyed sharing my west coast experiences with them; I wondered, in fact, if maybe people got tired of hearing about them. On afternoon shifts during supper break, I would talk to the other guys at work about my dream, of going back out west to become a fisherman. I would get a lot of strange looks and jokes about my aspirations. They must have thought I was quite the dreamer, but that didn't bother me; I now had a goal. I could not see myself working at Westinghouse all my life. Many had, and I gave them credit for it, but it was just not for me.

Over a nine month period I saved up $2500. That was quite a feat at the time at $4.00/hour, but having a sense of direction now, for the first time in my life, seemed to curb my urge to spend money on other things. My friend, Chris Taylor and I had stayed in touch occasionally during my stay in Hamilton. He let me know what was happening on the west coast; wild oysters were the big thing, he said, picking and then selling them was apparently good money. This was about a year before oyster leases and farms would start up on the BC coast.

For $400 dollars I bought a little 1964 blue Ford Falcon and decided that when I left this time I would drive across the country; up until now it had always been the train. I remember Mom telling me, "You've bought a lemon, but I liked the car anyway. In June 1973 I decided it was a good time to leave. Looking back, I am grateful for the support my parents gave me during that period of my life; without their help things could have been more difficult. True, like all families, my parents and I had our share of ups and downs but we managed to always get through them. Really, I had lots to be thankful for. With a somewhat heavy heart I started on my way west once again, not knowing at the time when or if I would return.

I slept in the car some nights but most often found a

campsite along the way where I could stretch out. The car's transmission gave up in Winnipeg; I had it fixed as cheaply as possible so it could get me to my destination. Even so, that repair put a dent in my savings. I arrived in Vancouver seven days later; looking back I guess I didn't waste too much time getting there. Having a plan in mind and a good eight track cassette sound system made the time pass quickly.

Candy Kid

The day after I arrived in Vancouver, I took the ferry to Victoria and headed up to Campbell River to meet up with Chris Taylor. Harvesting oysters and, of course, fishing boats filled a lot of our conversation. He had talked to a buyer in Sooke by the name of Harry, who ran an oyster plant with his son, Ed. Harry had flown over some of the coast and said there was evidence of lots of oysters. They needed people to go and get them. It all sounded pretty exciting for me. We would need a boat and financing of course. A fairly good boat was selling for around $5,000 and up. Anything less could mean you were only purchasing a headache; putting more money into repairs than you could make. And believe me, as I would learn over the years, boats need a lot of attention and have to be maintained regularly.

I met Chris's girlfriend, Diana, who also seemed to like the idea of being on the water and together the three of us went boat hunting. We drove up and down Vancouver Island looking for what would suit our needs and eventually, after a week of looking, found what we wanted. It had been lying under our noses all along, tied to the government wharf in Campbell River. She was 36 feet long, a double ender painted black with red and white trim. The deck and hatch cover were painted a bright green and those colours seemed to suit her name, *Candy Kid*. She had a six cylinder Perkins diesel for power and a large 8"x 8" timber that crossed her beam just back of the hatch cover. Cables ran from the ends of that timber to the bow of the boat. This set-up acted as an area to tow from, as the *Candy Kid* had a log salvage licence as well. This meant you could beachcomb for logs on shore, or take those adrift in the open sea. Once enough logs were gathered up, they could be towed to a booming area where they would be measured. Salvaged logs were paid for by the lumber company. It was a good secondary option for us, making the package even more attractive. The *Candy Kid* was selling for $4500.

I had my $1500 in savings still and Diana had $1500. Chris borrowed his share and by pooling our resources, we had enough to purchase the boat. It had great potential for what we wanted to do. We phoned the number on a "For Sale" sign that was in the window and shortly thereafter, with a little bit of paperwork, we were the proud owners of the *Candy Kid*. There was a lot for me to learn, I really knew very little about boats and what drove them through the water. Chris was better at wrenching than I was and he sort of took over the job of chief engineer; we were all pretty green, though. There is a large learning curve when you decide to make your living from the water and it never seems to end. This I would come to realize many years later.

We were now ready to go but before leaving I had to find a place to store my car. Fortunately for me one of the fellows I had logged with offered to let me park it at his place. It would be one less thing to worry about. I drove it there with my well-travelled "Dayton" cork logging boots locked in the trunk and turned the keys over to him. I said my farewells then, not knowing when I would be back.

Two days later and a week after purchasing her, we boarded the *Candy Kid* and left Campbell River en route to Jervis Inlet. I did not even know where the place was but kind of had the idea it was on the mainland shore somewhere. So Chris was not only the engineer, he also became the skipper.

This was something else! It was our first venture together on the open ocean and the sea was glassy calm. We had sure picked a good day for weather and it definitely made the journey more pleasant. Sooke Oyster Co. had made arrangements to meet us in Saltery Bay with a log barge we'd need for our operation, a necessary item. Saltery Bay is a small place with a government wharf located where Hwy 101 meets the water. There is a ferry dock there as well, the boat ride being your access north from here: a continuation of the Sunshine Coast Highway. Powell River is the next big town located further up on the other side of the inlet.

On schedule, the log float was there for us. The barge was basically a collection of large logs joined together lengthwise with boom chain. It had two logs cabled fore and aft which ran crossways to help hold it together. The log float would be what we'd tow behind us for many months to come, it would carry the cargo, oysters. However, we were soon to discover that finding oysters by water was not as easy as it may have first seemed.

Oyster Picking Days

Harry said there were lots of oysters up the inlet and, seeing it from the air, it was probably true. We scanned our old nautical chart trying to find ideal places to look and hopefully connect to spots that would match up with where he had spotted good productive areas. Small bays with sandy, gravelly bottoms were ideal; many places we found had oysters alright but on a closer look at low tide discovered there was not enough for a load. A load constituted about 300 sacks at 80-100 pounds per bag; a fair pile of oysters. We were paid $2.75 per sack; that was the deal. We eventually found enough for a load at the head of Hotham Sound.

We anchored the *Candy Kid* in the quiet bay and waited for the tide to drop. Often low tide would come during the night so we'd take Coleman lanterns onto the beach to help us see what we were doing. Fortunately the first low tide came just before dark and we were able see a lot more with the naked eye. The buyers did not want oysters that were too small so we tried to pick only healthy looking, medium-to-large ones; no rocks and no empty shells. Any oysters clinging to rocks we just left. We had been given 300 empty, large burlap sacks and into those we collected the oysters.

We would look for a large concentration, open up the end of the bag with one hand and toss the oysters in with the other. Once a sack was full we'd placed it upright, grab another and start again. Every now and again we would have to straighten up and stretch our backs. On a normal tide we would have 2-3 hours to collect and stack our product, before the tide started to come back in to shore. As darkness came upon us we'd to fire up the lanterns and this really changed the picture. The glow of the light on the beach certainly slowed us down, as vision was reduced to a much smaller area. As the tide crept back in we would move farther up the beach. Once the tide was too high, we would jump back into our small skiff and head back to the boat. That would be it for the night. A warm drink and sandwiches would put a fitting end to the day. We discussed how many sacks were picked and there always seemed to be a little competition going on as to who had done the most. We slept well that night, each of us crammed into our own little corner of the boat; if the tide was good in the morning we might be able to collect some more.

Oyster picking definitely hinged on the tides and we really had to plan each trip around them. When the tidal changes were small we stayed tied to the dock. On this, our first trip, we'd picked a good set of tides to work on. While waiting for the water to recede one afternoon, I decided to go fishing on a nearby reef. I threw out a cod jig and in two pulls I managed to catch a 17 pound red snapper. What a thrill! It made for a nice meal that night.

The next tide that evening saw us filling our last sack; now we would wait for high tide in the morning and then begin the tedious task of loading the float. Finally the water was high enough so Chris and I pike-poled the float towards the shore, directing the barge over to one of the many submerged oyster piles. We had put the sacks into groups of ten to twenty on the beach. Hovering just over the top of the pile was ideal as it would mean less distance to pull them up from the bottom. One of us would snag a sack with the hook on the pike-pole and raise it to the surface. Then Chris and I would each grab an end and hoist it onto the raft, piling them in neat rows. Pulling full 100 pound wet sacks from the water was no easy task and we had to watch our backs. In about three to four hours we were all loaded up. We adjusted some of the weight forward when we discovered that the back end of the float was about two feet under water. With the barge now more on an even keel, we hooked up to the *Candy Kid* and made ready to tow our load back to Saltery Bay. It was just before dark when got underway.

The loaded barge proved to be a lot of weight for our little six-cylinder Perkins diesel to pull. We made very slow progress but the weather was again on our side. Although these were fairly sheltered waters, the outflow winds could get fairly brisk. I remember it being a beautiful star-filled, clear cool night. We had our Coleman stove going on the *Candy Kid*'s hatch cover outside, and we sat and gorged ourselves on more fresh fish and boiled potatoes. We were all feeling satisfied and proud of our first trip, a little weary, but very happy.

We'd arranged to meet Ed the next day. He showed up on time in his large flat deck truck. We positioned the float at the end of a boat ramp so that he could back down for the quickest and easiest unloading. It would still take about two hours. Time was fairly critical here as there was a ferry to catch and also he did not want the oysters to be out of the water for too long. After doing a tally on the number of sacks we had, Ed wrote us a cheque and told us to phone him the next day. Finally, our first money in a while!

We cashed the cheque in the nearest town and picked up some supplies. Diana, being vegetarian, picked up fresh vegetables for a salad to enjoy, along with a little red wine. Chris and I bought two huge steaks, some beer and the necessary barbecue materials. We each had our different ways of celebrating. I have to laugh a little looking back; our preference in eating probably offended Diana a bit. We never converted her to eating meat but I must thank her for changing my diet around somewhat; as time passed by it seemed I became more aware of and selective in my choice of foods. It was, after all, a period when there was a growing awareness about better diet. More salad and whole wheat bread were supposedly not all that bad for you.

Next day we phoned Ed to see how everything went but the news was not great. We were told the oysters would have to be re-seeded in Sooke, so they could flush themselves out. An inspection had found some pollutants in the oysters and they were not ready for the marketplace. This was common practice and a very necessary part of the process designed to protect all.

The two deliveries we eventually made from that same area had the same problem. We never asked for any particulars on what was wrong, although in hindsight we should have. It was nothing we'd done, but something that was correctable in time as oysters were capable of cleansing themselves out. It did however affect our paycheck, as there was a charge to handle the product twice. The cost was fifty cents a sack to cover the time it took to re-seed and re-pick the oysters, a drop to $2.25 a bag.

We stayed tied up for one more day but left early the next morning to explore another area close by. We cruised around several small islands and checked out many coves looking for beaches that would have enough oysters to make a load. It was really an adventure being your own free person without a time clock or anyone else to answer to.

It was nearing the middle of summer, that time of year when oysters spawn. The warm water temperature brings on this cycle in their lives and they become softer and milkier inside the shell; making them not the best for eating. Winter is when they are in their firmest and most edible period. The warmer months of the year also can bring on "Red Tide." Oysters must not be eaten at this time as the paralytic algae can have a severe affect when consumed. Red Tide could be seen during the day and the Department of Fisheries would post warnings when spotted in areas: "No eating of clams or oysters due to paralytic shellfish poisoning". The problem was it could come and go during the night and you could not tell if the oysters had ingested it. It would not hurt the oysters, but at this time of year it was best not to eat the product, especially in the Gulf of Georgia where the algae bloom was most common.

It could show up quite suddenly and signs were then posted on the beaches affected to warn the public of the danger. To date we had seen no warnings in our area nor had we seen any sign of it on the water. It was, however, reassuring to know that all oysters are checked before going to market.

After a day or two of looking we came upon a promising site between Hardy and the Nelson Islands. We headed back to Saltery Bay and picked up our log barge. There was a favorable tide for oyster picking the next night so we had a day to get ready. The next morning we idled out in the direction of our new spot and I say "idled" quite literally, as we tried to keep our fuel expenses to a minimum. It was already becoming apparent to us that we were not going to make a bundle of money in this line of work.

We chose a nice secluded anchorage near the beach and waited for the tide to fall. This would be a midnight pick as the ideal low tides had moved along in the day. It was dark when we rowed our skiff in toward shore. The night was very still; not a sound. Only the crunch of our skiff grinding up onto shore broke the silence. We fumbled around a little bit until the lanterns were lit; this done we held them up high to see where the most oysters were located. There was the now familiar and almost eerie shadows cast from the glow of light that reflected from the rocks and trees further up the beach. Often we would think we saw movement but it was usually the light playing tricks on our eyes. Those shadows never amounted to anything, but they always managed to toy with our imaginations.

Oyster picking at this spot did not seem as good as we had hoped it would be; on closer examination there were a lot of empty shells, but it was not that bad. We worked hard and tied off our sacks before the tide came in at 3:00 am, then we sleepily rowed back out to the *Candy Kid*. Tides were not good during the day so we slept in a little that morning. It took three low tides to get a load for delivery but we managed it and then connected with Ed once again back in Saltery Bay. The first trip had taken all the guess work out of what needed to be done and our second delivery day went smoothly.

By now in two trips we had scoured most of Jervis Inlet and the surrounding islands. Things were not looking as good as we had hoped due to the amount of volume that was needed in order to make it work. It was looking like it was time to move out of this area altogether. There was only one direction to go from here and that was north.

In early September, we left Saltery Bay and travelled through Malaspina Strait towards Powell River. On the way we picked up another load of oysters at Northeast Point on Texada Island. This we delivered to Powell River, where the ferry from Vancouver Island arrives. This location made it easy for our buyer to pick up our product. Unfortunately this load turned out to have the same problem as the first two and the oysters had to be re-seeded. They were let go in Baynes Sound, a stretch of water between Denman Island and Vancouver Island. The hard work and ongoing disappointments were getting frustrating to say the least.

As we ventured through this part of the coast we discovered that the more promising oyster grounds had already been staked out as lease areas. This meant they were basically closed to any outside activity, us included. It was to be the future in the oyster business as individuals or companies could, upon application and acceptance through the Department of Fisheries and Oceans, now hold an area as their private spot.

Dave Holland

This arrangement eventually proved to be better for the stock in general, as it encouraged more of a farm mentality and a brighter future for the oyster industry. For us, however, it meant our oyster picking days were numbered.

Our travels took us past Harwood and Savary Island and eventually led us to a place that would, without knowing it at the time, change the course of our lives. As we passed a small point of land on an afternoon cruise, off to our right side, the small community of Lund came into view.

From the water, you can readily spot a large structure, that being the Lund Hotel, with a few homes and buildings on either side of it. There was a fuel dock that extended out onto the water directly in front of the hotel and to the right of that was a floating breakwater that protected the government tie up floats in behind. All in all it was a picturesque setting that had a peaceful, quiet out-of-the-way feeling about it.

We secured our log barge to the pilings near the fuel dock then tied the *Candy Kid* up beside it for the time being. After shutting the motor off we walked up a ramp to the large wooden platform above. This area housed a small shed that contained oil drums and other items relating to the fuel dock's operation. In the opposite corner was a large winch used to load and off-load vessel supplies. The highway ended here, where the asphalt met the timbers of the platform.

Yes, Lund is as far north as you can go on this coastal highway, which makes its start away down south in Mexico. Basically it was the end of the road. This was further confirmed when we noticed a large welcome sign there that proudly stated "Welcome to Lund, BC, the end of Highway 101." In later years the local community scratched out the word "end" and replaced it with "start" as it could be viewed either way.

Past the sign another 20 steps and you were officially pretty much in downtown Lund. As we would learn, the Lund Hotel was the centre of the community. It housed a pub in front, which faced the water, and along its side, facing the harbour, was a dining room, café, store and post office. The second floor of the hotel had rooms to rent for those who were visiting or staying. Directly across the road from the café door was the ramp way leading to the government dock with a boat launch right beside it.

On the other side of the hotel was a long float that led to a single story concrete building. The sign above it said Lund Marine. There were quite a few boats tied to that float with the far side of it being an access lane to a dry dock for haul out. This family run business was owned by Jens Sorensen. He had his three sons, Marvin, Mark and Dan, employed there; all were heavy duty mechanics. In time it would turn out to be handy for us to have a supply and service facility so close for repairs when needed.

Being our first time to Lund, we decided that a beer would taste good so Chris and I went to the pub, while Diana decided to check out the rest of the town by herself. The pub was fairly small but comfortable inside. There was a juke box near a pool table in an area separate from where we were sitting. The pub, we found out later, was referred to often as the "Lund Living Room" and it definitely had that cozy feeling to it. We took a table near a big window in front that offered a view of the scene outside. What a picture it was, the land in front opened up to a view of the water with Savary and Hernando Islands in the distance. Beyond that we could see the mountains of Vancouver Island in the background.

The year was 1974. Long hair and beards were common with the younger crowd and there seemed to be a healthy mixture of both present.

One of the first people to greet us was a fellow named Rudy who we found out owned *Sea Truck II*, a self-powered landing barge that delivered supplies to the surrounding islands in the area, a job he really enjoyed. I believe it was Chris who eventually gave him the handle "Rudy Yah-hoody". It is now many years later and once in a while we still keep in touch with each other.

Chris loved to play pool so we walked up to the bar and while he put his name on the board to challenge the winner on the table, I ordered two glasses. The bartender turned to me and said, "And what do you want?"

"Two beers, please," I replied. He turned, kind of mumbling to himself, but at the same time he seemed to be almost hiding a grin beneath his somewhat harsh exterior. The bartender's name was Bill and I kind of liked him immediately. I sensed he was trying to bait me into a reaction of some kind but I did not respond because I wasn't yet sure what type of reaction would be suitable. It was like we were going through a feeling-each-other-out process. As I got to know him better, I came to realize that he could be a little gruff in his approach but could also at times be totally the opposite. I think Bill loved to get a reaction or response from people. It made his job more enjoyable by keeping everyone on their toes.

It's funny in life how you can relate more to some people

and not others but I definitely connected with Bill from the start. He was in his late fifties then and I'm sure he had seen many people and things come and go. He told me one time that he played for the Chicago Blackhawks in the NHL. I am sure he had other interesting stories he could have shared but when he was at work his conversations were short.

Bill had a way of leaning against the bar and putting his arms straight out to the side with both hands clenched on the counter top. With his head cocked ever so slightly to the side he'd look directly at you from his side of the counter. Then out would come, "Can I help you, madam?" or to a girl, "Good day, sir." You could either laugh or, if your sense of humor was limited, go back to your seat and shake your head. Most people took it well because, well, that was Bill. There were times I would tease him back but I learned that you had to know when. It was all in the timing and presentation. Bill ran the place and he was master of the bar.

I handed Chris his beer and we talked to several people. Of course, everyone was wondering who these new faces in town were. No one entered or left Lund without being noticed, especially from this vantage point. The talk eventually came around to oysters and we learned that there were lots of them further up the coast in Desolation Sound. There was even an oyster plant close by in a place called Okeover Inlet. It all sounded very promising, especially after a few more beers.

The next day we left the barge behind and set off in the boat only. We headed north through a narrow channel that passed by the Ragged Islands then emerged out the other side where again the water opened up. We passed by Bliss Landing and then rounded Sarah Point, the gateway to Desolation Sound.

Dave Holland

Our destination was Okeover Arm which was the next stop over. In a relatively short time we arrived at a fairly wide channel that marked the entry way to the inlet. We had decided to pay a visit to the oyster plant there and found the place exactly as it had been described to us. We tied the *Candy Kid* up to a small float in front of the plant. As it turned out, the operation had recently changed hands and a fellow named Greg and his wife were the new owners. Greg was a little older than us and a graduate of UBC. He'd wanted to try the oyster business as a fresh new line of work. Certainly in this remote part of the coast it was probably, if nothing else, a welcome relief from city life. Along with the plant, Greg had the rights to the oyster lease at Mary's Point, located at the southern tip of Cortez Island, approximately a two hour boat ride away. Greg needed someone who could deliver product and that is where he felt we could come in. We agreed to a dollar per sack as the delivered price. It was less than what we would get for wild oysters but it would be a lot less stressful overall. The product was there and we would not have to burn all that fuel and time looking for some pot of gold that had so far eluded us.

We made an agreement and left feeling somewhat more secure than when we had arrived. On the way back to Lund we decided to have a look at the area we would be working and see for ourselves if it was as good as it sounded. At first glance we could see that Mary's Point offered a good sheltered anchorage for the boat. Upon further investigation it became apparent that the actual size of the oyster lease was huge. There was a sand bar above the high tide mark that fell off on either side to a large gravel beach more predominately on the northern slope, where it formed a large horseshoe. When we rowed our skiff to shore the bottom revealed solid oysters underneath. It was an oyster picker's dream. We had never seen anything so prolific; there was enough product here to keep us busy for a while. Greg would tell us when a load was needed and we would plan a trip when the tides were most suitable to his specified time frame.

In the meantime, we phoned our original buyer in Sooke, Ed, and told him of our situation. He was fine with it. I think all of us realized by now that the wild oyster plan had not worked out as well as we had hoped. He thanked us for our effort in trying and wished us all the best. As far as the log barge went, he said he really had no more use for it and we agreed to pay him a small amount of money to purchase the float once we'd made our first delivery.

We set to work immediately as there were good low tides during the night and the plant was in need of oysters. Lighting our lanterns on shore revealed solid oysters pretty much all around us; we were walking on them in our gumboots as we looked for the ideal place to start. It was easy picking and we found that we could fill a hundred pound sack in about an eight foot radius. On previous beaches, we'd get a portion of oysters in one spot then drag our partially filled sack behind until we found another place in which to fill it. Not here! We each picked 50 bags in a small area on the first night and within two tides we had a load.

After our first delivery, we tied up to the small government dock directly across the way, leaving the barge safely behind at the oyster plant anchored to the beach. At that time there was a restaurant at the top of the dock called Roo's Resort. The restaurant was the end of a three mile gravel road that meandered out to the main highway which went either north to Lund or south to Powell River. Lund was only five miles away and we chose this more accessible community to get supplies when we needed them. Besides, our first impression had left us with a good feeling about the place; it kind of felt like home. We were soon to become officially "locals" and delivered a load of oysters whenever the plant needed one.

At this time, I believe the small, cramped quarters of the *Candy Kid* were beginning to wear on all of us. Really, there was not much room for three people. Diana decided to look for a house to rent and a short time later, she and Chris moved into a small cabin about one mile up the highway from downtown Lund. I would often stay at Diana and Chris's when I was ashore; a hot shower, television and a good stereo system were a welcome relief from the boat.

It did not take long to meet many of the people who lived in the Lund area and, to them, we became known as the "oyster pickers". Diana soon landed a waitressing job in the Lund Hotel dining room, while Chris and I looked after the oyster end of things ourselves. I remember Diana's job helped with their rent, as our income was still somewhat sporadic.

The three of us by now had realized that we probably wouldn't be making our fortune in this line of work, but we also knew it could have been worse. We were young and full of optimism then, and our lives had settled into somewhat of a regular routine. As the winter of 1974 moved slowly along, we picked many oysters; there were places on the lease where the crop was definitely starting to look thin. I was becoming restless and beginning to wonder where we would go from here. I think Chris and Diana were feeling the same. Little did I know it at the time, but the winds of change were starting to blow and a brand new opportunity was about to unfold, in my life.

2

Shoal Bay.

"Antique Dave"

Most of the time there seemed to be a steady flow of boats moving in and out of the Lund Harbour. Some were based there permanently but of course a large number would come and go. There were fishing boats, log salvage vessels, tugs and landing barges. It was a fairly busy little place. At the time the *Candy Kid* crew would be placed in the come and go category.

Returning to the harbour one afternoon from an oyster delivery, something caught my eye as we tied to the government wharf. There, moored at the very back of the far finger, was a small blue and white fish boat. *It has great lines*, I thought, and walked over to have a closer look.

The name painted in black letters on either side of the bow was *Antique*. A For Sale sign taped to the window simply read $5500, with a phone number beside it. The sliding door was locked. I glanced through the small oval window and could see the steering wheel and a seat located over top of the motor inside. I stepped back onto the dock and paced off the length, estimating it to be at about 28 feet and approximately 7 feet wide.

There was a small cockpit area in the stern of the boat where you could stand. In the middle of this area was the rudder stock, with a removable steel bar extending from it that enabled you to steer the vessel. Directly in front of here was an open box for landing fish, with a two spool gurdie system on either side; they were connected by a long belt. The port side had a large transmission box where a pulley-driven shaft connected to the one side of the belt system. The other side of the box had a longer shaft that ran through to the back of the cabin where it disappeared inside. I really had no idea how any of this worked, where it went or what it did, but at that point this did not matter. The boat that I had been dreaming of for some time was right here in front of me.

It was now nearing the end of January 1975. Our oyster trips were fewer and further apart. It was time, the three of us decided, to put the *Candy Kid* up for sale. It had been a great experience overall but we mutually agreed it was time to move on. Each of us had our own ideas and plans about what we wanted to do next. I wanted to go salmon fishing with my own boat, Diana was happy with her land job working in the Lund Hotel, and Chris was talking about being a guide for sports fishing; it was something he had done before in Campbell River. Just a short time later we found a buyer and recovered the money we had originally invested in her. I had my $1500 dollars back, and could now make the first steps toward purchasing the *Antique*.

It turned out the owner of the boat was a man by the name of Art Powell. He lived in one of the small houses that surrounded Lund Harbour, with a lady named Millie and another fisherman, by the name of Henry Miettinen. I had met and talked to them before in the Lund Hotel over a beer; they always sat in one of the tables to the right of the entrance. That, it seemed, was where the more established locals liked to sit. I'd often join them, listening to their stories, and they would also lend an ear to mine. I had direction in my life and that, I believe, went a long way with them.

Lund was such a small town that I think Art already knew of my aspirations and dreams to fish with my own boat. It wasn't long before we sat down to share a beer and talk about the *Antique*. As it turned out the *Antique* was a Category B licensed vessel, meaning it was only licensed to fish for a designated period of time. The boat had four seasons remaining on its current fishing privilege, after which the license would expire. At that point you would have to purchase a category "A" license in order to continue fishing that particular vessel. An "A" license was good for life. Four years seemed like an eternity to me at the time, so the limitation of the current license had no bearing on my thought process.

Art and I agreed to get together the next morning and go over the *Antique* from bow to stern. A rebuilt four cylinder Ford diesel had recently been installed and that was a bonus. The engine would be fairly new and more economical to run. The boat needed some work but nothing that appeared to be major. I trusted Art in what he had to say and after a couple of hours we shook hands and made a gentlemen's agreement that I would buy the boat for $5000. I had my $1500 in the bank and would need to borrow another $3500 to finish the deal.

At this stage of my life I had never dealt with a bank and I was somewhat at a loss for what to do or say. I also hadn't established a credit rating for myself. I made an appointment with the Bank of Commerce in Powell River, where I had an account, and was told that in two days I would find out whether I could move forward with my dream. It was at this time that Henry stepped into the picture.

I had only recently met him but it seemed that we had a mutual understanding and liking for each other from the start. I think he got a kick out of me being so green. I was the new young fellow in the industry and I enjoyed listening to his fishing stories. One of the things I would often hear and certainly learn over the coming years was that you must *always respect the ocean.* I first heard this advice from Henry and truer words than those would be hard to find. Little did I know then how this wisdom might serve me in the years ahead. Without me asking or saying anything, Henry offered to go to the bank with me on the big day and speak in my favour with the loans people.

Henry was from a large fishing family that was one of the earliest to settle in the Lund area. He was in his early sixties at the time; a large somewhat quiet man until it came time to talking about boats or fishing. He had his own 36 foot vessel the *Pair a Dice*. It was a combination boat, meaning it could either troll or gillnet. So here I was, about to hopefully make my start in an industry that Henry had worked in for much of his life. We may have been miles apart in some ways but we did have that common connection.

It seemed like forever to me then, but the day arrived when I had my appointment with the bank. I was nervous and, looking back, it must have been quite a picture for the bank manager when Henry and I walked through the door of his office. There was Henry, the well-established local fisherman sporting a brown fedora and a new shirt held tight to his chest by his always present pair of suspenders. Beside him was me, a young man of 23, with shoulder length hair; I was dressed in a new plaid long-sleeved shirt and the newest pair of blue jeans I had in my possession.

I nervously explained my situation and the bank manager listened quietly. I was young, ambitious and full of dreams; not always what a banker wants to hear. When I had finished, he carefully looked at his paperwork. Henry then broke the silence and said, "I believe this young fellow has what it takes to make it, I hope you give him the chance."

I am not sure that without Henry's support that day I would have been approved for the loan, but I got it. When I reflect back now, it was definitely one of those special moments that can happen in a person's life and one in mine I have never forgotten. I will always be grateful to him for that.

After we had signed all the necessary papers I gave Art his cheque and at that point I became the proud owner of the *Antique*. I moved all of my worldly possessions on board, which didn't amount to much, but the boat had now become my home as well as my source of income. Back then the fishing season opened for salmon on April 15th. I had a little over a month and half to get ready; not a lot of time.

On board the *Antique* was a little standing area just inside the sliding door; from here a two-step ladder led to below. There was a small cupboard area that held utensils, cups and plates, with shelves beside and near the bow for storing my clothes. The other side housed a small bunk and wood stove, which was the source of heat. The stove was located between the sleeping quarters and engine. Everything was right there for sure; not a lot of room, but it would do.

The first night on board I lit the stove; it was still early March and cool. The wood stove worked fine, getting almost too hot, but cooled off quickly when it burned down; I'd then have to get up to re-stoke it. I was going from hot to cold all night long with little sleep. Eventually I hooked up an electric heater to the dock power and this solved the problem. There was no water tank or sink either so I purchased two plastic five gallon containers with a valve on each. These I put outside the door and on the side of the boat for easy access. I used that water for drinking and washing up on board but there was also access to fresh water from the dock as well; with that availability I managed fine.

It certainly was not the Grand Hotel but at the time that seemed irrelevant to me. I had become used to life on board a boat and knew that you had to put up with some of the discomforts. The *Antique* was no exception. I made up a work order list of things that had to be done. At the time it was only 10 dollars to renew the "B" license but I did need to get vessel insurance for my protection and the bank's. The bank had given me an extra $1000 dollars to cover these start-up costs. Fortunately at the time, the government offered what was called the Fishing Vessel Insurance Plan. It was for me the most affordable way to go so I set up an appointment for later in the week. The inspector would try to cover every port within a certain timeframe, so myself, along with many others in Lund, did our best to comply.

The items they wanted to see included an overall clean and tidy boat, adequate bilge pumps, both electric and manual, and in general a safe working vessel. I set to work addressing these items right away and with co-operation from the weather I was able to sand and paint the checkers; this was the landing area where the fish were first brought onboard. There were also covering boards over this area to keep the sun off the fish until you delivered your catch to the buyer. Any areas that came in contact with fish, like my checkers, had to be painted with a white non-toxic marine paint that I purchased from Lund Marine. I had no fish hold to pack iced fish, so that was not an issue here. The *Antique* was strictly a day troller.

I had three bilge pumps, one manual and two electric automatic ones, one under the engine and one in the hold area of the boat. The pump in the hold would come on quite regularly as she had a few areas where water wanted to seep in, not an uncommon thing for wooden boats of her vintage and something I had to keep a close watch on. On the bow behind the tie up cleat was a small plastic milk container box and in it was some rope and chain that was connected to a small anchor. The vessel was not set up too well for regular anchoring but it would always do in an emergency. There were two life jackets tucked away below in the fo'c's'le[1] of the boat and a life ring on top of the cabin outside.

I gave the *Antique* a good scrub down from bow to stern and did a final once-over before the inspection officer arrived that day. He was on time and I remember his name was Neil. After a couple of other boats were completed, I was next in line. He asked several questions, and then went through a list of check points. All in all it took about a half hour and I was done. My boat passed inspection and after signing some paper work, I was good to go. It was a big step out of the way.

There were many other things that still needed to be done. Painting the hull could wait until warmer weather, so I focused my attention on the mechanical end of things. I tightened the chain steering system and replaced a couple of rusted blocks. Inside the wheelhouse, the only electronics I had was an Ekolite Flasher Sounder. There were no radio phones for on water communications; she was pretty simple and basic in many ways. There was a little seat above the motor and the valve cover acted as a footrest. The engine was right there, very open and consequently very loud. A small steering wheel mounted in front of the captain's chair pretty much summed up the rest of the

---

[1] The fo'c's'le is the forward part of a ship below deck, usually used as the crew's living quarters.

cabin area. To the left of the steering assembly and attached to the wooden dash were three important gauges that showed the engine temperature, oil pressure and rpm's of the motor. The throttle cable control was located to the right side of the wheel.

I constantly asked Art and Henry questions about all sorts of things to do with the boat and as always they were very helpful. Art ran me through the start-up procedure. "First you check oil levels in the engine and gear every morning and also check the water level in the motor," he said. "Then and only then, do you turn the key to start up," he added. To get at these things I would remove the small portable stairway; this opened up access to the side of the engine that housed the dipsticks for checking oil levels. Directly in back of the stairs was a large 8D battery for starting the engine; it also housed the connections to the sounder and bilge pumps.

The small floor area just inside the wheelhouse had a steel bar directly to the left of your foot that would allow me to manually engage the gear. Pulling it back moved the boat forward and pushing it ahead put the boat in reverse. The gear was a Capital with a 2½:1 reduction ratio; the back of the gear housed a coupling to which the drive shaft was connected. It all seemed so simple tied to the dock, but I wasn't so sure how I would feel as I needed to get used to the boat out on the water.

The next morning looked like a good time for a trial run, there was little boat traffic and it was flat calm with no wind. I did my pre-trip checks then fired up the engine, giving her a few minutes warm-up before untying from the dock. This done, I pushed the bow away from the wharf, entered the cabin, then eased the boat into forward and idled out of the harbour.

Nervously I pointed the bow towards the entranceway near the breakwater and headed the boat into open waters. I pulled the lever back on the throttle cable control; the engine responded and I gained speed through the water. I let the engine idle back down and put the boat in and out of gear, making sure that everything was working properly. I did this in forward and reverse so I'd get used to the boat's response.

After about a half hour of this I felt confident enough to take her back to the dock. It all seemed to be working fine. I moved the steering wheel back and forth to be sure everything was free on the way in. But still I felt a little anxious so I slowed the boat's engine down to as low as it could go. As I approached my spot at the wharf I eased the boat into neutral and cranked the wheel hard over, letting her glide into the dock. I then put her into reverse to allow the stern to move into a perfect position, but I misjudged slightly. The stern instead bounced into the dock first. I quickly jumped onto the float to try and hold her in place then realized she was still in reverse. Back into the cabin I raced, taking the boat out of gear. After a couple of minutes, all three lines were secured and she was there, safely tied to the dock. I looked around as subtly as possible to see how much attention I had brought to myself and fortunately it looked like the coast was clear. There was no one around. Still I was pretty sure this little moment in time had not gone totally unnoticed. I went down below and shut the motor off. To anyone else, that first short trip out might not have seemed like much, but for me it was a big step in building my confidence. It was also the first time I had the opportunity of running my own boat, on my own. It was not a perfect start, yet I felt a sense of satisfaction come over me; it seemed like another small hurdle out of the way.

As the days rolled along, I got a better feel for the boat, her quirks and her movements. While I started to feel more comfortable with everything, there were still plenty of items on my list that needed to be done. Mother Nature was weaving her magic as spring was only around the corner. Schools of herring travelled in and out of the harbour. The water was cold and crystal clear so that anything moving below the boat was easy to spot. The morning air was crisp and the days slowly grew longer.

With the new season approaching came a sense of anticipation and excitement. What kind of year would it be? In time I came to realize that you could never really know what the next season would bring; there certainly were no guarantees in this business. At this point, I just wanted this one to get started.

The next thing on my list was fishing gear, a necessity; you had to have it. The boat did not come with much; there were some leads or "cannonballs". They are attached to the end of each of the wire trolling lines and basically sink the wire line straight down into the water. There were also two styrofoam floats or "pigs" as they're called. They are designed to clip onto the trolling line and when set back a certain distance prevent that line from tangling with the one forward. There were a few spoons and hooks in one of the shelves down below but not much else. The steel line was already wound on to the gurdies, although it looked to be fairly old as there was visible evidence of breaks and a few splices.

Gear was unknown territory to me and the subject raised at least two questions: Where does a guy get all these items and what should he buy? I really did not have a clue so I relied on information from some of the other fishermen. But the trouble was each and every person had their own favorite set-up and system, consequently this got very confusing. The bottom line was that gear would be something I'd probably have to figure out on my own. Fishermen would willingly tell you *some* things but trade secrets were kept to oneself. After all, when the gun went off we were all in competition with each other and everyone wanted to be "high boat". So I accepted only the information that was offered and was careful not to pry.

By now my funds were getting low so I knew I would have to watch my spending. Most established fishermen had a line of credit set up at one of the gear stores for starting up the year and I could see why. I needed quite a few important items and I made up a list: flashers, hoochies, plugs, hooks, cannonballs, fishing line or perlon, and trolling snaps, just to name a few. The closest big supplier of fishing gear was John Redden Net Co. in Vancouver. I phoned them first before going to the big city to be sure I would be able to access a line of credit. At that time, as long as you had a boat, most places welcomed your business. Usually any new fishermen could open an account. I was given verbal clearance over the phone and promised to have the required paper work ready when I arrived at their store.

Several of us from Lund made the trip to Vancouver the next day. We shared the vehicle and ferry costs to get there and knew it would be an all-day adventure with two ferries and a couple of drives in between. We arrived at the store around noon and immediately set about our business. After I completed the credit application form I was cleared to go and I started to look around the place. The place was huge. Where to start? There was row upon row of fishing gear with one entire aisle devoted to spoons and another designated exclusively to plugs. I could easily get carried away here but I realized I had to stay within reason and especially within budget. It would not take long for things to add up. I stuck to my list of important items but there was so many of each type to pick through. One of the store employees suggested a few items that worked well and were big sellers, especially in the Gulf of Georgia where I would be starting out. I looked through the hoochie section and that also took up a whole aisle. There were hundreds of types and colors to choose from and I picked out several packages, each packet containing ten of each. Hoochies are towed behind a flasher. They are made of plastic and imitate small squid, octopus, cuttlefish and shrimp, some of the things salmon liked to eat. The flasher has two purposes when moving through the water, it imitates a feeding salmon and also creates action on the hoochie which can entice a fish to bite.

I would eventually learn what gear was "hot" and what was not. But again that would only come with experience, the one thing that at the moment, I did not have.

Selecting gear and catching fish is a science unto itself. Hoochies, for example, have clear bellies or white. Either can work better in different conditions. Water clarity has a huge impact on what colour works the best to attract fish: should I prepare for clear

hoochie

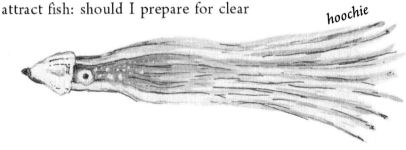

or cloudy conditions? To play it safe, I decided to stay with some basic, proven producers. Plugs that imitated herring also came in all sizes and colours and I picked up a couple of boxes of those, with six plugs in each box.

I needed fishing line. It came in small rolls or spools of different lengths. The "pound test" was marked on the spool and indicated the line's strength, or breaking point. It was rated by a number from 40 pound test to 100 pound test. The fishing line, called perlon, was a clear nylon product that blended in well with the water, making it invisible to the fish. There were also trolling snaps that attached all of these types of gear to the steel line. I needed both of these items. And so on it went for at least two hours that day.

When, finally, all of us were done, I had purchased the equivalent of what amounted to a couple of small cardboard boxes full of gear. I had also bought four 25 pound leads or cannonballs and a cleaning knife. In money terms this all amounted to about $500. Those small boxes really added up.

Henry teased me when we got back to Lund, "You're a big time spender and you haven't caught a fish," he said. What could I say?

By this time we were into the first week of April and the season was set to open in only ten days. I spent a lot of time organizing the boat, putting things together so that when I was out there fishing and needed something, I could find it quickly. I ordered fuel and oil filters for the engine from Lund Marine. Art gave me a hand installing them so I was familiar with what was involved; I changed oil at the same time so all was ready mechanically.

I was to learn that a big part of catching spring salmon was being able to hug the rocks on the bottom with your leads, thereby "scratching" your gear along the edges and cliffs below. Those were the places where salmon often would feed and where they'd have a hiding place from their predators. That is where my depth sounder came into play. It was mounted on the small dash directly in front of the door so I could watch it when sitting in the cabin yet still see it from the stern of the boat. A red blip on top marked the surface and the same blip on the oval screen would indicate the depth of water I was in. The scale read from 0 to 70 fathoms, a fathom being six feet. I went out several times to get used to where the shallow spots were and to familiarize myself with this "flasher" sounder. I had to have the dial adjusted properly, turning it up when the water got deeper and the other way when the bottom came up. Because I would be fishing the 30 fathom edge I set the sounder so it worked to perfection at that depth.

A couple of days before the opening I had everything ready to go, or so I thought. There was still the actual gear to tie up and with the help of a few locals I quickly learned how to tie a fisherman's knot. There were three loops around the finger, back through the hole, moisten with your mouth, pull slowly tight and trim off the excess line with your cutters. It took me several attempts to get it right so the knot would not slip or be loose. I eventually got it and learned that moistening the line prevented it from chafing against itself and weakening. This prevented a possible break when a fish struck. This connection was used at the swivel of your trolling snap and also at the other end of the line where it was connected to another swivel on a piece of gear.

My "B" license arrived in the mail. I attached those "B" tabs to the Canada fisheries plates that were mounted on either side of the *Antique's* wheelhouse and was now ready to go. The Fisheries plates were on all vessels and clearly visible to any fisheries officers who may be about. Your letter, be it an "A" or in my case "B", indicated what your vessel was licenced or allowed to fish for. Around this time a fisheries officer arrived in Lund to inspect fish holds and any landing areas for salmon. As all of us had been ready for this next necessary procedure for quite a while by then, my boat passed and with that I was officially cleared to go.

Finally, it was one day before the opening of the 1975 season and everything seemed ready. Chris came down and we spent the afternoon going over my boat. Being a former guide, we both talked about fishing at length and what type of gear salmon might most likely want to bite. We shared a few beers together and, as usual, had a few laughs. It helped to put me at ease, and that was something I needed just then. I went to bed at 9:00 pm with the alarm clock set, only to lay awake thinking most of the night; I slept little.

I was up bright and eager at 4:00 a.m. First I went through the start-up procedure and when done, turned the key to fire up the engine. It was still dark when I went out on deck to wash my face and wake up a little. Daylight seemed to come at around 4:30 and shortly before then I untied the boat and idled out of the harbour. There was the usual light offshore morning breeze but the sea was, as the saying goes, flat calm. There were half a dozen other boats doing the same. I turned the boat north in the direction of the Ragged

Islands, only minutes away, and made ready to start my day's fishing.

Staying away from the shallows, and when the sounder read 70 fathoms, I engaged the power take off on the motor inside that provided the drive to run the gurdies. The gurdies are the drums around which the trolling wire is spooled and a lever on the back side of each one, when engaged forward, allows you to let the line out or bring it back in. When you were done with one line you pulled the lever back to disengage that gurdie and then moved on to the next one. There were four gurdies on the *Antique,* so I had four lines to deal with. I moved to the stern of the boat and put the transmission drive in reverse mode. Then I engaged the lever and started to lower the first line into the water, snapping on the first piece of gear on the mark that was above the lead. The steel trolling line I used had sets of two brass sleeves crimped on at regular intervals every 2½ fathoms (15 feet). It was between those brass sleeves that the trolling snap was attached to the wire line. Each trolling snap, of course, had a piece of gear attached to it a certain distance back. In my case it could either be a flasher or plug. The small brass sleeves or "marks" on the line spaced the gear and kept each piece riding within the small gap between the two marks. This separation prevented each piece of gear from tangling with the one below or above it.

I put a plug on the bottom mark then missed a space before snapping on the next piece of gear which was a flasher and hoochie. I then counted off ten marks, lowering the line down to a depth of twenty-five fathoms. At that point I snapped on the float or pig that would take the line back to whatever distance behind the boat that I felt was safe and ideal. Next I attached a "donut" that would take the line out to the spring at the end of the trolling pole, thereby spreading the gear out. This connection was referred to as the "tag line" and when all the weight had been taken up by the spring and it had extended a little, that line was now in place.

This back float was referred to as the "pig" line and it would separate itself from the forward lead, called the deep or main line. Without that spacing the lines would obviously end up in major tangles. It took me about half an hour to put out all four lines and between steering the boat and watching the sounder I eventually had everything ready and in place. I put three pieces of gear on each of the two deep lines, which were set at thirty fathoms. I ran two on each of the back lines that I'd set at twenty-five fathoms.

Back in the wheelhouse I kept my eyes on the water ahead and also kept a close watch on the sounder. I'd occasionally look at the end of the poles, watching for any movement on the springs that would indicate a fish had struck a lure. Each spring on the trolling poles had a bell on it so you could also hear if anything had hit the gear. However, from inside the *Antique* all I could hear was the diesel engine purring away. By now it was getting lighter and the sun started to show on the horizon. Other boats were fishing inside of me, working the edge, and after a couple of trips back and forth with no results from my own tack I started to work my way in a little closer. The tack here was fairly short. A small rock was a landmark where I would slowly turn out towards the bottom end of the Ragged Islands and eventually head the boat back in the direction of

67

Lund. At the southern end of the tack I turned at a point of land off Sevilla Island and headed back up the beach, to start all over again. There and back was roughly forty-five minutes.

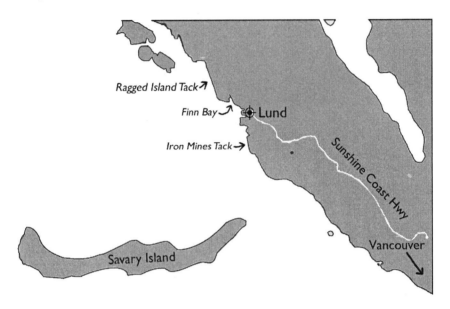

This went on until 11:00 o'clock and then the other boats pulled their gear aboard and headed back to Lund. I had constantly checked my gear after every pass but the result was always the same: no fish. Shortly after the other boats had left, I brought everything in and did the same. The local boats tied up directly, bypassing the fish buying station. That was not a good sign. As it turned out high boat that first day had caught three fish and everyone else had at least landed one. For such poor results it was common practice to tie up first and then just carry your fish over to the buyer. This was referred to at the time as a "finger delivery". I would have been happy with a finger delivery but such was not the case for me that morning.

Oh well, that's how it goes, I thought to myself. I did feel somewhat satisfied in that everything worked properly and my confidence level had gone up a little, fish or no fish. The common practice in the gulf was to fish the "morning bite", come back into the dock around noon, then go back out at 4:00 pm to try the "night" bite. This met with the same result as the morning, nothing. However, I did become more familiar with the grounds and would be ready to give 'er the next day. Little did I know at the time how long this slow fishing period was about to last.

No Fish

Activity picked up in Lund as more and more boats from out of town arrived on the scene. Many of them used Lund as a stopping place to "wet their gear" and be sure all was working fine before heading to the north coast where any problems would be harder to resolve due to isolation. These vessels were often from Vancouver but some also called Southern Vancouver Island their home. It was a fun crowd, and me, being the newcomer, would listen to the stories they had to tell. A few of them were also relatively new to fishing, having maybe only started the previous year while others had much more experience. This knowledge, combined with the anticipation and uncertainty of what lay ahead, brought a boisterous feeling to the air. No matter how long we had been at this, we all felt the same exuberance and excitement that came with the start of a new fishing season. The mood was upbeat.

I remember some of the boats and skippers quite vividly. There was Bruce on the *Ern*, John on the *Cathy Bell*, Paul on the *Essie T.*, Judy and her deckhand Annie on the *Adella P.* Annie always wore a pair of hoochies as earrings and every day they would be a different colour. It was a diverse crowd of individuals but a friendlier or more helpful group of people would be hard to find.

Every day, usually in the late afternoon, a large black packer called the *Norpac 11* would arrive in Lund to pick up what fish had been delivered and drop off fresh ice to the small buying station in the harbour. The boat would leave Vancouver early every day, pick up fish throughout the Gulf of Georgia and then return each night for delivery to the main plant in Vancouver. This made a long day for the *Norpac* crew but this service kept a constant supply of fresh fish available at market. Up until this point, my only delivery had been a two pound rock cod. *That* fish would not feed many people. Chuck, who ran the Lund fish camp, was in touch with the packer every second day and he passed on all the current news. From him we learned that all through the gulf fishing was poor; it was slow everywhere.

Days rolled by and though I'd fished the *Antique* every one of those days, I still had not caught a salmon. It wasn't much better for others. The high boat of the day might have 2-3 fish. *1975... What a year to start*, I thought to myself. My enthusiasm waned but never diminished entirely because each new day brought hope of something better.

While my general attitude overall remained high, my finances began to dwindle. I had only a small amount of money left from my loan. Don and Mary, who owned the Lund Hotel and store, were good enough to let me charge the odd meal in the restaurant and groceries from the store. They knew I was trying but at this rate I was slowly going backwards. I had fuel to worry about also. All this in combination was starting to dampen my spirits a little.

Knowing that I had to do something different, I started getting more aggressive on the tack. I began cutting in closer to the rock ledges that made up the shoreline in the Ragged Islands. Whatever fish that were being caught came from that particular area. I was getting better at reading my Ekolite flasher sound and by watching the beach for landmarks, started to know when to turn the boat in or out from shore. *There has to be one here for me,* I thought, trying to be the eternal optimist.

One morning I thought I had a fish. The spring on the end of my starboard trolling pole moved slightly but then stretched out hard to the maximum. The boat started to list over then suddenly jolted back. I had hooked something all right, as the saying goes; British Columbia! My cannonball had caught bottom and broken away. The lost lead was another expense to add to the growing list. In my urgency I was a little overly aggressive and ventured too close to the rocky edge, and it cost me. It was another step in the learning curve. I quickly pulled the line in, fastened on another cannonball, then lowered the line back down and continued about the morning's business.

Turning at the end of the tack I moved farther outside of the edge and continued back up the shoreline. Again there was a small tug on one of the pole's springs as I straightened the boat out after the turn. Could it be? I engaged the transmission that drove the gurdies and slowly started to bring the line up. I stared over the side until the first piece of gear came to the surface, then unsnapped it from the line and coiled it into the boat. With that complete I watched as the next piece of gear approached the surface. The mainline started to move back and forth in the water; I reached down and grabbed the line, there was tugging motion and it felt heavy in my hand. I saw a flash of silver. The fish darted back and forth and I struggled to control its movement. I was being extra careful to not pull back too hard, worried I could tear the hook out of the fish's mouth. But then suddenly the fish bolted for the stern of the boat. The line went slack in my hands as I failed to keep him under control and then I felt a small thud through the floorboards as the propeller did its damage. My first salmon, in its panic to be free, swam into the propeller; the line went tight again as I pulled in what was left. I had caught a fish at last, even though it was only half of one. It still made for a good dinner that night.

April turned into May and while some of the boats started to leave the Lund area, others would arrive. There seemed to be a constant flow. Many combination boats, being both troll and gillnet vessels, would briefly stop for the night. Some tried their luck the next morning trolling but many just kept going, heading up coast for gillnet openings in the central and northern areas.

I'll never forget the day that John on the *R.W.* and Len and Marian, on the *Starlite,* motored into Lund. They arrived late one afternoon for a stopover following their day's run from their home port of Ladysmith, on Southern Vancouver Island.

I was tied to the dock, working in the stern of my boat and getting ready for what I hoped would be a "night bite". John came over to my boat to check on this newcomer and to see what I was up to. He was a fairly short man in his early sixties. I was drawn to the white cap on his head that he wore cocked off to the side in his own distinct manner. It was his halibut hat or "highliner's cap". It seemed like a permanent part of his attire and it would be rare that I ever saw him without it on.

I had been tying up some new gear when he walked up and quietly studied the knot I was using. "I can show you a quicker and better way to do that," he said. By only going around my finger twice, it turned out to be easier, faster and as strong as what I'd become used to. Without realizing it then, John and I had made a connection; it was the first moment of a friendship that would last for many years. Quite often, whenever something broke down or suddenly went wrong, it seemed John was there to try and help in some way. Eventually, he became almost like a second father to me.

However, the learning *how* to catch fish was another matter; that I had to figure out on my own and besides, my stubborn pride would not have allowed it any other way. It was probably much the same internal process that John himself had to go through many years prior.

There were other fishermen that offered their knowledge. Paul on the *Essie T.* showed me the proper way to splice the seven strand 1/16" thick steel trolling wire. This was especially helpful as the wire on the *Antique* was getting weak and worn in places and always in need of attention. Some of the Lund locals started to offer suggestions as well, such as trying new grounds. Peter Wells showed me the tack at Keefer Rock but a morning's effort yielded nothing but a few cod. Peter and his fishing partner, Dave, were building a 52 foot fiberglass troller at a shipyard in Vancouver. Now in their third fishing year, they seemed miles ahead of their time with this project, as there were few larger trollers on the coast then.

Another Lund local, Bob, decided one day he would come out with me on the *Antique* and see what I was up to. Bob had fished the previous year and I welcomed any knowledge he could offer. He decided we should try the tack south of Lund for the morning. The shoreline there was cliff like and fell away straight down to the ocean. There was a full forty fathoms of water close to shore. A rusty coloured stain marked parts of the grey rock on shore and hence the tack was named the "Iron Mines". We hugged the shoreline all morning with no results. Around 1:00 o'clock we angled out a little and started a final turn back to Lund. With our checkers still empty it was time to pull our gear and head back in.

I watched as Bob started to bring in the last line on his side of the boat. As it started up from the deep he suddenly yelled out, "We got a fish!" The steel line jerked back and forth as he slowly brought the gear to the surface. I stood beside him in the stern staring anxiously into the water behind the boat. Suddenly there was a big flash of silver as the salmon broke the surface. It was wild and very lively. Bob yelled, "I'm lowering the line back down to let him cool off." This technique was used for bigger fish in hopes of calming them down and wearing them out a little; it made it easier to land them in the boat. With this done, he turned to me and said, "Get me your gaff".

"Gaff?" I said quizzically. A feeling of sudden panic gripped me and I guess I must have given him a blank look.

"You don't have one!" he said in disbelief. "Well I need something!"

Of all things to have not purchased at the gear store in Vancouver, a gaff, something to actually bring a fish aboard with, was at this moment the worst. This fish was too big to throw into the checkers on hook and line alone as we ran the risk of tearing the hook from its mouth.

I bolted out of the stern and rummaged through the wheelhouse. What could I use? My adrenaline was working overtime. I found a piece of a broken hockey stick down below and, using an old rusty handsaw, quickly cut it into a two-foot length. Then I grabbed a large standard screwdriver and bent the steel part so that it formed a hook shape, sort of. With some twine I quickly lashed the two pieces together. There! A gaff! This done, I hurried back to the stern and handed it to Bob. He looked at it and shook his head but said nothing. Slowly he brought the line back up; the fish was still on and it had calmed down considerably.

I stood beside him in the stern and watched closely, not wanting to miss a thing. He guided the fish slowly up to the side of the boat, quickly slid the gaff under the gill flap then flipped the fish out of the water, over his right shoulder and into the boat. At the very moment that fish was sailing through the air toward the checkers, my makeshift gaff fell apart. Yet amazingly enough, the salmon and what was left of the gaff, still wound up in my small landing box on board. The fish flopped wildly about until Bob grabbed the piece of wooden hockey stick and knocked him on the head. It then lay still and I stared at my first spring salmon. What a beauty!

Neither of us said a word and I quietly watched as Bob showed me the proper way to clean a fish. I had no wash down pump so when he was done, he picked up the fish firmly in its now-cleaned gill area, and lowered it over the side to wash away any remnants that needed cleaning, both on the outer side and inside the cavity of the fish.

At that moment I remember thinking, *"Don't drop him."* When he was finished, Bob placed the fish gently into the checkers. All the while this excitement had been going on, the *Antique* continued idling along without a second thought about it from me, and now we were directly in front of Lund. With the gear stowed away, I hoisted the trolling poles back into the crosstree, then proudly headed the boat towards the harbour.

I weighed the fish at the buying station: it was fourteen pounds dressed out; a nice size fish for the gulf at this time of year. I decided my first delivery should go to Don and Mary at the hotel, with the proceeds going towards my account. By now, the word was out and had travelled through the small community that "Antique Dave" had caught a fish! "No way!" must have been, I'm sure, how some of the locals thought.

Well, three weeks to catch my first salmon certainly was not how I envisioned my first year to have started, but so it did. I carried my fish up the dock and presented it to Don and Mary in the Lund Pub. People stood around and clapped; there were pats on the back and even the odd picture taken. It was a big day for me and I felt a little bit like a local hero; this moment of celebration seemed to have helped make the long wait a little more worthwhile. A genuine feeling of warmth and camaraderie revolved around times like these; that's what it was like in Lund and many small communities back then.

After the excitement, and when all was said and done, Bob and I sat down and enjoyed a beer together, on me. He always claimed that he had caught the fish but in return I would remind him that it was my boat. All was better two days later when the Packer delivered my new gaff to the fish buying station in Lund. I was now ready for anything.

The term was "scratch fishing" when slow like this, and as we neared the end of May there was little sign of it improving. Salmon fishing was starting to remind me, in some ways, of our oyster picking days. It could be a long time between pay checks.

Boats continued to pass by, using Lund as only a brief stopover place, a stepping stone to northern waters. It was not long before John and Len also left, hoping for better things in the Port Hardy area.

At this point, four weeks into the season, my impatience was growing daily. I could not afford to stay with this much longer. However, I still had some important things that needed doing before I could go anywhere, the annual haul out being first on the list. There was a small marine ways and yard on Sevilla Island, a piece of fairly sheltered land that marked the entrance into Finn Bay. This marine yard was owned by George Bone, a local shipwright who went about his daily work with a patience acquired by very few. He was a quiet man in his seventies and very good at his craft. At the time he had a young apprentice working with him whose name was Bill McKee. I approached George and Bill about getting my boat hauled out and after a quick look at the tide book they confirmed it would work in two days' time.

When that day arrived and on the morning tide, I prepared for my first haul-out. I guided the *Antique* into position and stopped her directly above a submerged wooden platform that would serve as her cradle when she was pulled up on land. Once she was in place, I secured her to the platform's two upright stanchions. This done, I shut the engine off. The platform sat on four small iron wheels that road on two steel tracks leading up to the high tide line. It was an arrangement very similar to a train track system, with a long steel cable connecting the trolley to a large engine-driven winch on shore. When all was ready and in place George and Bill fired up the Chrysler Crown motor, engaged the winch and up the beach the *Antique* slowly went. In about five minutes, my boat and I were high and dry.

I climbed down to survey the bottom of the boat once it was securely in place. Outside of a good scrubbing all seemed to be in order. Bill checked the cooling pipes to the engine, the propeller and of course, the zincs or what was left of them. I had noticed a trickle of water coming in around the stern area; it was most noticeable when the boat was at running speed. It was just a dribble, but it still bothered me. I set about scrubbing the bottom of the hull with the stiff bristled brush I had purchased.

The algae, barnacles and mussels stubbornly stuck to the planks but with a little elbow grease the bottom was soon clean and ready for a fresh coat of anti-fouling copper paint.

In moments between my vigorous work, I asked George and Bill many questions. "What is this for?" and "Is this anything to worry about?" and so on. After the boat had dried somewhat, I applied a fresh coat of copper paint, being careful to keep a nice even waterline. She had to look good.

The reddish brown copper paint bordered her main hull colour, which was light blue. Because of the accessibility, I painted the blue shade from the waterline up to the guard rails on both sides as well. The copper paint would keep the algae at bay for a while and deter any toredo worms from eating into the underwater wood planking. Toredo worms are saltwater creatures that can do major damage to unpainted wood, leading to all kinds of problems if undetected. Bill power sanded the propeller until it was clean and shiny, then replaced all the old zincs with new ones.

Zincs are described as "sacrificial" because they will eventually erode. Their job is to stop the reaction or charge between the saltwater and the metals below decks. Without zincs on the hull, electrolysis can occur and it can eat away at the metal in cooling pipes, propellers and your shaft; not a good thing. Bill then re-caulked the planking in the stern area but had to use oakum, a heavier and thicker form of cotton that is used on wooden boats. The oakum is pounded in between the seams of the boat's planks. It swells when wet, keeping everything tight in the process. The *Antique*, being a fairly old vessel, needed this product, especially in the stern where I'd noticed the leaking and where things had opened up a little more over time. Once the oakum was in place Bill cemented over the newly reworked seam and when it was dry enough I applied copper paint over top. By the end of the day the bottom of the boat was as good as new, in my opinion, and ready to go back in the water with a big annual job out of the way and some peace of mind for her skipper.

There were other things that needed attention, like the rigging. I made sure the turnbuckles weren't seized and the stay lines were tightened up. Of course I would have to finish painting the boat topsides as well, but overall I felt she was now ready for most anything that lay ahead.

It was nearing the end of May and with growing confidence, I started to expand my boundaries further. I tried other places, like Sarah Point an hour north of Lund, and Bakers Pass, which is located at the bottom end of Cortez Island. It could be a good spot to catch small Coho salmon or blue backs as they were commonly known. I trolled up and down both sides of the pass one morning but the fish were scarce. By noon with the gear back on board I ran through a narrow channel close by that eventually opened up to a small cove, named Cortez Bay. There was a general store there with a small float in front where you could dock your boat, as well as a small fish buying station close by. *How convenient,* I thought, and so I delivered my meager morning's catch there. Inside this little cove were several other trollers tied to their own floats. A ramp to shore was their access to maybe seven or eight homes that dotted the shoreline. I remember the names of a few of those boats. The *Liz* and the *Lady Jane* are two that come to mind. These local fishermen would day-fish the waters nearby, sell their catch and be at home within minutes. What a set-up! And there was even the beautiful scenery on top of it. Lund of course offered much the same, but this area seemed even more isolated and serene.

I would discover many places like this along the inside waters of the Gulf of Georgia. Many of the people living in these picturesque little places had other work besides fishing. For some of them, fishing was their summer job and often a husband and wife would venture out on the ocean to try and round out their yearly income this way. "Ma and Pa operations" were a common nickname for boats like these and it seemed to me a great way to spend the summer months. A person could make a little money, and at the very least, have lots of seafood stored up for the winter months ahead. Let's face it, canned salmon of any kind is always tough to beat.

Another spot I visited north of Lund was a place called Bliss Landing or Sharpe's Bay, as many of the locals referred to it. I met Reg and Eileen Sharpe in Lund one day. They were getting some supplies for their boat in preparation for the trip north to Port Hardy. Bliss Landing was a good name for this beautiful out of the way place they called home. They lived in a small house that was very close to the beach and sold fuel from a small dock at the water's edge. It was only a half an hour north of Lund, and offered a sheltered little cove where they could also permanently moor their 36 foot troller the *Sharpe's Bay*.

By now the slow fishing in the gulf was wearing on me and I knew I would soon have to move on to better grounds. As the newcomer here, I asked the Sharpes a few questions about the trip north to Port Hardy. I was curious, having heard stories from other people about navigating those waters and everyone had similar tales to tell. It seemed to be a place where having some prior experience was key, and like all the others, they suggested using the buddy system. If anything went wrong, having another boat travelling with you was the safest way to go.

There are two passages to the north from Lund. One is along the Vancouver Island side of the Gulf of Georgia, from Campbell River up, and is called Seymour Narrows. You have to travel across the gulf first to access this route. It is a little longer journey but probably the more commonly travelled, especially for larger vessels. The other, more scenic sheltered route from Lund, is on the mainland side, through three sets of smaller tidal areas, Gillard Pass, Green Point and Wellbore Channel. Travelling this particular route is fine, as long as you access these areas either one hour before or one hour after slack tide. In both of these access routes to the North Coast, the tide will flood to the south, and ebb to the north. Of course, everyone had their own personal horror stories around navigating these waters over the years. The currents run strong through these narrower channels, as I had found out in my much earlier swimming experience at Race Point, when I was almost swept away after jumping into the water.

Anywhere tidal water is being squeezed from a wider area to smaller can wreak a lot of havoc, with swift water, whirlpools and back eddies. As long as travel was done during the proper time frame, you would be alright. However, at times the pressure would be on, and captains might push a bit to be able to reach their destination sooner rather than later; those could be potentially dangerous decisions when made.

The three sets of rapids, Gillard Pass, Green Point and Wellbore Channel, took about three and a half hours total to navigate. Being a little early of course helped if the tide was with you. The currents in all three places can reach seven to ten knots at peak, depending on how big the tides are at the time.

The normal route, I was told, for a boat capable of a six or seven knot speed, was to leave Lund four hours before tide change, get through Gillard Pass and then tie up at a place called Shoal Bay, about an hour's run further along. There was a dock and store there. You could spend the night and get the morning's tide change the next day. From there you could leave two hours before slack tide, and that would get you safely through Green Point Rapids and Wellbore Channel.

All this information, combined with some of the stories I'd listened to from other fishermen, produced a large knot in my stomach. The more I heard, the worse I felt. Of course, fishermen are renowned for exaggerating their tales, as a good story usually commands a bigger audience, but still, I was growing increasingly anxious about making this journey. There was no way I was going alone.

It was now into the first week of June and fishing had remained spotty. I couldn't stay in the Lund area any longer; I was starving here and it was time to leave. I had met several other fishermen who agreed. There was Paul on the *Essie T*, Norman on the *Cygnet* and Dan on the *Seamaid*. The *Seamaid* had an Easthope engine in it; and Dan would hand crank the flywheel to start it. I found it amazing to see this done, as well as hear the sound this motor made when it was running. It was a very quiet engine, with its famous "ka-put, ka-put" tune that echoed through a "wet exhaust" pipe. Paul knew Reg and Eileen on the *Sharpe's Bay* so the five of us decided to travel north together and we'd leave on the most favourable tide the following day. All had more years fishing than me, so I was the green man of the group.

When Art heard that I was getting ready to leave Lund, he asked me if I had any money, to which I replied, "No".

"You can't travel north without money," he said and then insisted I take the twenty dollar bill he offered me. It was a very nice gesture from Art and not at all expected; I thanked him for the loan and with that, I said my farewells to him, Millie, and of course, Henry.

They wished me well and each of them gave me some kind of last minute advice. They were much like doting parents whose child was just heading out the door. I would miss them, if only for the three months I'd be gone. "See you in the fall," I said. With Henry's words *respect the ocean* ringing in my ears, I headed down to the *Antique* to get ready for my departure the next day.

Northern Venture

Even before daylight, I was up and ready for an early start. I checked the motor over, making sure coolant and oil levels were fine. The fuel tank was full and I had enough food for three day's travel. Food did not amount to much. I had a loaf of bread, peanut butter, sardines and a can of tuna. *What's with the canned fish?* I joked with myself, *I've gotta be a little more optimistic.* All of these supplies I kept in my small cupboard below. Finally, everything seemed ready to go. Chris came down to see me off and after having a coffee together and the usual few laughs, I felt more at ease.

It was a beautiful sunny day; a great day to be travelling. At about 10:00 am, I untied the lines from the dock, Chris gave the bow a push out, and I was on my way. I took my place behind the other boats with a feeling of confidence. I was heading out on another adventure, and once I was under way, I realized that I was actually looking forward to it. I guess in some ways it's the not knowing what lies ahead and the anticipation of what might happen that made what I was doing for a living exciting. I truly enjoyed it.

Once we were all on our way, there were lots of things for me to do besides looking at the scenery. I constantly kept a close eye on the gauges to make sure they indicated that all was well with the motor and gear. I also had to look out for stray floating logs and, of course, deadheads. They can lay just below the surface on end vertically. Hitting one of those, if it was big enough, could seriously damage your boat or propeller.

It was turning into a hot day so I dropped open the two small cabin windows in the front. They were normally secured in place by small wooden wedges. With them opened, a cool breeze passed through the wheelhouse and gave me a slightly clearer view ahead.

Before too long we passed Sarah Point and Desolation Sound then entered the start of Lewis Channel. Once through this stretch of water it opened up somewhat. I could see the entrance to the first set of rapids ahead, in the forefront, blending in somewhat with the mountains and the trees behind. As we got closer, I could make out the white marker beacon at the bottom of Stuart Island that marked the beginning of Yuculta Rapids. Right on time we entered the rapids about an hour before slack tide; we would now get a small push northward, on the last of the flood.

I nervously gripped the steering wheel as the stories I had previously heard rushed back to me. I watched Paul's boat ahead of me start to rock gently back and forth, and then mine did the same as the currents boiled to the surface all around us. I could readily see why you would not want to be here at the wrong time. It was almost slack water and yet there was still plenty of current, back eddies and evidence of small whirlpools on the surface.

About ten minutes in to the pass, we took a hard left and headed toward a marker light on shore signalling the entrance to Gillard Pass, the narrowest stretch of water in this area. This is where you want to be at the turn of the tide. During peak tides, the entranceway is often marked by a large whirlpool, the kind that stories grew from, but for now we were right on the mark, time wise. Nonetheless my boat was still getting pushed around and had to keep a firm grip on the small steering wheel. The *Antique* would at times seem to almost stand still, then it would surge forward a little before it would again bob back and forth.

Quickly we were through this section, and then the pass opens up a bit. The turbulence settled right down, giving us a short break before another short and narrow stretch just ahead.

The Dent Island marker light signalled the end of the

Yuculta Rapids ahead, but just prior to that point the water narrows right down again at a place referred to as Devil's Hole. This is another spot where a large whirlpool can occur during maximum tide. By now, however, it was almost slack water and we passed through this last little stretch quite easily.

The channel then widens and for the next hour we quietly motored along. We soon rounded a second point that opened up to a fairly small cove on the left. This was Shoal Bay. Since there was a large government dock here, we decided to tie up for a couple hours. It would break up the trip and allow us to stretch our legs. We could catch the final two to three hours of the ebb and be safely at our first day's destination, Forward Harbour.

I really had an immediate attraction for Shoal Bay and in the years to come, it would be one of my favorite places to stop and spend a night. This little place on the BC coast has a rich history. It first started up in 1895, when gold was mined from the surrounding hills. Eventually that slowed down and it then became a logging and fishing site in the 1920's. There was even a school at one point, until the coastal population grew in other areas and people moved to less isolated places, like Campbell River.

All-in-all, Shoal Bay has a beautiful setting. Looking north from the dock, sharp mountains surround a large inlet named Phillips Arm and behind you in the opposite direction is a low, grassy shoreline with a little creek that drains into the ocean. At the time there was an older wooden supply store about halfway down a long, wide-timbered boardwalk that started at the top of the stairway from the dock and ran to the beach. Here was where the main lodge was and it housed a restaurant and lounge area inside.

The old store at Shoal Bay.

It amazed me somewhat then, but even more so in later years, how these little remote, out-of-the-way places always seemed to have in stock just what you might happen to need. With sales being seasonal and most of the travellers having stocked up before leaving home, these little operations could never carry a huge inventory, but when you found yourself in need of something every so often, some small store in the remotest of places wherever you might be, would have it. It understandably cost more money but that was of little consequence when you were able to find exactly what you needed.

We left Shoal Bay two and a half hours before the next tide

change and, with a gentle push from the last of the ebb tide, we slid through Green Point Rapids. This relatively short stretch of water is shaped like an elongated upside down S. We passed by the entrance to Lochborough Inlet and then turned right into Wellbore Channel. There can be a large whirlpool present here where the channel narrows near the far end, but we arrived pretty much at slack water so it was virtually non-existent.

Having all the rapids behind us was a great relief. A short distance later we entered the very calm and sheltered waters of Forward Harbour, a relatively small inlet that was a common stop-over for many vessels. We tied to a can buoy in the harbour for the night, which was a bonus for me with my anchor gear being not the best. There were four of these mooring buoys here that were installed by Transport Canada in certain areas along the coast, Forward Harbour being one of them. They, in turn, were securely anchored to the ocean floor and very much a convenience for all vessels, as they saved you from having to anchor.

To this point the route is truly the scenic way to travel along the inside passage. As well, the waters are fairly sheltered all through the area, only getting a little choppy during outflow winds from the local inlets.

The next morning I once again went through the start-up ritual, and everything seemed fine. I added one litre of hd30 motor oil then I fired the engine up. It seemed to take a little longer to come to life but it did. I noticed that the water temperature was cooler here than further south in the Strait of Georgia. This coolness also reflected in the air temperature. Two or three degrees in the ocean can make quite a difference overall; it was no longer t-shirt weather in the early morning here, that's for sure.

The sky was grey with a layer of low cloud overhead, but there was no wind; the air was still. Those that had a VHF radio phone onboard said the forecast on the weather channel sounded good. After a quick coffee we all untied and idled out into the strait.

Once through this short stretch of water, we entered the bottom end of Sunderland Channel and in about an hour's run we cruised by Port Neville. This marked the entrance into a wider, more open stretch of water called Johnstone Straits. From here, Port Hardy was about 10 hours away. It would be a long time to sit and hold the steering wheel. Every so often I'd stand up off the little seat and stretch. I'd walk out on deck but never stayed there for long as I always wanted to be looking forward, making sure all was clear ahead.

At about the halfway point up the straits, Norman signaled me to get closer to his boat. He yelled through a megaphone that he and Dan were going to cut in by the Broken Islands, a slightly more sheltered route to Port Hardy. Another reason for their decision was that Dan had been having a bit of engine trouble. I had a chart covering this more inland area, and so I decided to tag along with them, Paul and Reg would carry on up through Johnstone Strait. Norman had a radio phone and he let the others know of our intentions. I idled up close beside the *Cygnet* and Norman gave me his spare megaphone so we could talk to each other from a distance. There was a light low-lying mist close to shore and I remember we followed closely behind the *Seamaid*.

We wandered a little off course and wound up getting fairly

close to a rocky shoreline that had a small cove nestled in behind it. My chart indicated this place was called Port Harvey. *That sounds an awful lot like Port Hardy*, I thought to myself. But from all that I'd heard about our destination, this was certainly not Port Hardy; there was nothing here.

A short while later we tied to the dock at a place called Minstrel Island. Dan took the opportunity to go over his motor. It sounded like a fuel problem so he changed his filter and in a short period of time had everything working well again. We were on our way having lost very little time and reckoned that we could still reach Port Hardy by late afternoon.

Around 2:00 pm we cruised past Alert Bay, Sointula and Port McNeil. A lighthouse ahead on Malcolm Point signaled the entrance to the open waters of Queen Charlotte Strait. Our destination from that point was about three or four hours away.

About two hours later and as we neared Round Island, I noticed that a little more water had gathered in the bilge under the motor. I had two automatic bilge pumps on board which were regularly coming on every fifteen minutes or so. They ran off of a single 8D battery, which was also used for starting the motor. Something was apparently wrong with the automatic pumps, so for the rest of the time I pumped water over the side manually. Fortunately the *Antique* also had a small, manual bilge pump behind the wheelhouse, so I wasn't going to sink.

Of course, with my boat being fairly old I had to expect some water to enter in places. Most of the seepage on the *Antique* came in where the rudder stock came through the hull at the stern. A concrete seal had been poured around the base of it but I could still see a small trickle of water entering, especially when the boat was at running speed. There was no leakage from the newly fixed oakum seams; this itself was a separate problem.

And so it was that I was hand pumping my bilge as I rounded Masterman Island, making my first grand entrance into Port Hardy. I was relieved somewhat, to say the least.

We idled past the Seafood's Fish plant and tied to the government float that was located the furthest in to the bay. It had already been a long day but I had to find out what was wrong with my boat. Both the slow start up and the bilge pump problem needed to be investigated. I shut the motor off and tried to re-start it, but it wouldn't go. I checked the battery terminals and cleaned them but that did not help.

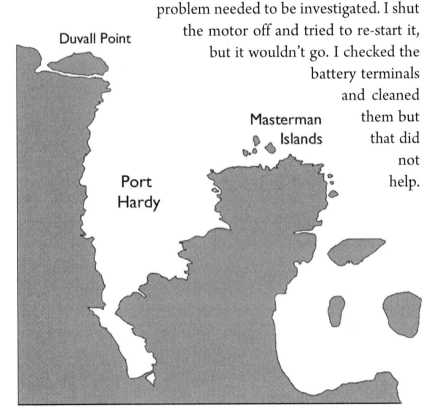

The general consensus, with some advice from the other skippers, was that I had a dead battery. I needed a new one, great! The twenty dollars Art had lent me was the only money in my possession and it would not be enough to cover such an expense. I had made it to Port Hardy alright but was now broken down with very little money.

John on the *R.W.* had seen us come into the harbour and came over to talk. After hearing of my situation, he suggested I go see Don Cruikshank, the head man at Seafood's. I had no other options. It was almost evening when I got there, but Don was still in his office. I introduced myself and explained my situation to him. He then opened a line of credit for me. In return I would sell my fish to Seafood's Product Fish Company. His generosity was a lifeline for me at the time and a tremendous relief. I could also charge my fuel and any necessary fishing gear as well, up to a certain point of course. This assistance would help get me through until fishing picked up. Don Cruikshank, as I would come to know, had a great connection with all of the fishermen and was very aware of their needs. His positive communication with everyone involved in the industry was definitely one of the reasons Seafood's Product Fish Company became so successful in the years to come.

The next day I went to Port Hardy Auto Parts and charged a battery to my Seafood's account. One hundred dollars later, with my new heavy duty D-8 marine battery installed in the boat, I was ready to go fishing.

At the base of the plant on a small float adjacent to the delivery dock was the Esso fuel station and gear store. It was run by a fellow named Rick. Always personable and helpful, Rick went about his business methodically despite a hectic schedule that saw a great number of people through the doors on a daily basis, especially during the height of the five month salmon season. But Rick always seemed to have time for his customers and this trait made him popular with everyone there. I fuelled up then, and purchased a chart of the local area that showed the surrounding islands and reefs from Hardy Bay to the mainland shore. This was an absolute must-have item, it was something during the course of an average fishing day you were constantly referring to.

With everything back in order I now felt recharged and ready to leave Port Hardy to go catch some fish! Unlike the Gulf of Georgia where it was common to fish a morning and evening bite, here in the north, depending on where you were, fishing was more of an all-day affair. As always, my friend John gave me a quick breakdown of where I should start and what to expect there. He had fished this area for many years and knew his stuff. He advised me to stay fairly close to him for a while, until I'd become familiar with the location and any new set of rules. Fisheries had large white triangle markers on land and you could not fish inside the imaginary line that connected the markers. Hardy Bay was one of these locations, with markers at Duval Point and Masterman Island, on either side of the bay. As long as you stayed outside of these areas you were alright. From the harbour to each of these places was about a half hour run and John suggested I start there.

Sure enough next morning, I was on the Duval Point tack. For my first day's fishing I basically put out all the gear that I'd used in the gulf. John was fishing across the way at Masterman

Island, and although he was a couple miles away, I could still make out his boat in the distance. That first day proved unproductive for me and I headed back in around 3:00 pm, very discouraged. John was heading in at the same time. I tied up near the fuel dock and watched his boat slide over to the delivery dock. Curious, I walked over to see him unload seven nice sized spring salmon, the biggest being around twenty-five pounds. He had a grin on his face and looked at me as if to say "What! You've never seen a fish before?" I guess my look said it all. So despite my own poor day there was fish in the area after all, and John's catch sparked in me some hope for tomorrow.

"They like spoons in this area," John said. I had mainly flashers with hoochies and I was also running the plugs that I'd used predominantly around Lund. With John's suggestion in mind I walked into the gear store and checked out the spoon section. There was a large selection. Wonder spoons, McKnight, Glendon Stuart, Tom Mack's and Eel spoons were only some of the name brands available. There were Coho wobblers in colours of blue, green, cerise, and yellow. Apart from the colourful Coho spoons, much of the stock was designed for spring salmon fishing, exactly what I was after at this time of year.

A box usually held a dozen spoons, and at two dollars apiece, they were not cheap. Rick suggested some popular brands, so I purchased two number 5 ½ Wonder Spoons, brass/chrome and two number 5 Tom Macks straight chrome. These were individual spoons, not boxes. *Let's not get carried away,* I thought, *At least not until I've caught enough fish to pay for these.* This would be a trade-off, however, as a common saying among fisherman then was: *You have to have lots of gear to catch lots of fish.* At this stage, though, I was leaning more toward the cheapening-out side.

The next morning I went back to Duval Point, determined to do better. There were signs of feed in the area and that could mean fish. I tried a different gear set up this time by putting out less gear on each of my four lines. The front, or deep lines, had a flasher, with a spoon and then a plug above that. On each of the back lines I had a flasher right above the lead and then a spoon on the next mark above. With everything out and my lines in the water I went to the wheelhouse to keep a close eye on the sounder and what was ahead. The tack I was working was relatively short. It took about fifteen minutes to go up the outer beach and the same to come back. A quick glance at the sounder showed I was in thirty fathoms of water; my gear was set at twenty fathoms so I knew I was alright for depth. Ideally here you want to hug the edge below at the depth your gear is set, or close to it, pretty much the same theory used in the gulf.

A quick glance at the sounder would show if the bottom was coming up, in which case I'd turn the boat out and away from the edge. At times, if the bottom rose steeply, I'd have to rev up the motor and this increase of speed would, in turn cause the lead cannonballs and the gear to rise up and ride over top of the obstacle. Once over the hump you could idle back down on your speed and the gear would settle back down to its normal depth. Often this maneuver enticed fish into biting as the change in speed gave different, life-like action to the pieces of gear and could excite the fish.

Other times, of course, if not watching closely enough, there was the possibility that your cannonball wouldn't lift high enough or fast enough and you could lose that lead. At seventy cents a pound back then, such a loss could get expensive. I used twenty-five pound leads on the front lines and twenty pounds on the back. Many experienced fishermen joined the wire line to the cannonballs with a brass spreader bar that opens up fairly easily if snagged. You then would lose the lead only. However I wasn't going to give up anything like that too easily, so my leads were securely fixed to the line with two hundred pound test green gangion twine. This extra strong connection would prove later on to be a costly mistake.

When fishing, I would continually glance at the ends of each trolling pole, back and forth, side to side, checking out the action of the springs and searching to see if a fish might have hit. You lived for the moment when the springs on the end of the poles would move in and out, indicating something had grabbed one of the hooks below. This back and forth head motion was why us trollers were often referred to as "swivel necks".

Looking ahead at one point, I noticed the steel stay line that connected the trolling poles to the front of the boat, had moved slightly. I looked out the side window to see the spring on the port deep line moving in and out and it was not just a minor tug. Moving quickly to the stern I made ready for some action. There was definitely a fish on the line, so I let it fight away for a while because I didn't want to bring him up too early. I placed my gaff in a good location for quick access, then engaged the gurdies and started to bring that line in slowly. That took the weight off the spring on the pole and the line started up directly beside the boat.

I could then see that the line was now moving back and forth as my catch was fighting to get free. I took off the first piece of gear. It was a plug with no tension on its line. I unsnapped it and coiled it into the boat. The next snap neared the surface and I stopped the line with the snap just below the waterline. Reaching down I grabbed the perlon: it was tight.

6" plug lure

I looked back to see a large flash of silver swimming off to the side of the boat. This salmon was bigger than anything I'd seen before. I pulled on the line and the fish pulled back. I had a quick glance over my shoulder to again make sure my gaff was in place, then slowly, hand-over-hand, started to bring the fish towards me. I got him halfway to the boat, leaving the slack perlon to lay in the water in case it wanted to go for a run. I'd been told that wrapping the line around my hand was not safe practice with larger fish especially. They are powerful and that perlon line can really cut deep into the skin if the fish decides to take off. And that is what this fish then decided to do.

It took a run straight away from the boat then jumped into the air trying to shake the hook out of his mouth. The line went tight and I cringed thinking the fish had broken free; but it hadn't. My heart was pounding. I grabbed the line and started the procedure all over again. This time I got him to the side of the boat. I turned to grab the gaff then took a fast, wild swing at the salmon's head but I missed. The glancing blow brushed off the side of its smooth head and only served to make him mad. Off it swam in a flash, now straight out from the side of the boat, tugging hard in short and fast motions. Amazingly the line held, even after that missed blow with the gaff. I figured on the initial run he was going to break the line for sure but he hadn't, and now the fish was beginning to show signs of tiring.

I had let the boat wander out to the deep a little so I could concentrate more on what I was doing with the fish without worrying about the edge or the depth. Again I started to bring the salmon back in towards the boat, hand-over-hand, slow and steady to keep him moving with an even tension on the line. At a distance of about seven feet I grabbed the gaff in my right hand and continued to bring him closer into my reach. In no time at all, it seemed, the fish was there. This time I swung the gaff and landed the hook in the gill flap and then with a quick flip I threw the fish over my right shoulder into the boat and landed him in the checkers. The fish went wild. I grabbed him around the tail for control and knocked him on the head with the back of the gaff, the fish quivered then grew still. I stared in awe. This salmon easily took up much of the space in my small box. I then removed the lure from the side of its mouth, it being the chrome number 5 Tom Mack spoon I had bought the day before. It had certainly paid for itself and then some as this fish must be over 25 lbs. What a beauty!

Spring salmon are the largest species of salmon. They have a rainbow sheen on their upper backs when they first come out of the water that blends into the silver sides of the fish. The characteristic black jaw and gum line along with the black dots on their back and tail finish marking this distinctive species of salmon. They are easily recognized for their size alone, the average in the Gulf of Georgia would at the most be eighteen to twenty pounds; my first "north coast" fish was a prize.

Untangling the line I returned my gear to the water, lowering the lead to its proper depth and made my way back to the tack. The rest of the day yielded another twenty pound spring, three Coho in the five to six pound range and two smaller springs weighing in at around ten pounds each. All in all, it was not a bad day. I cleaned the fish while I was still out on the grounds so they lay washed and gutted in the checkers, on display and ready to unload. The bite seemed over by 2:00 o'clock and I made my way back to Port Hardy to sell, feeling much better than the previous day. It felt good knowing I had made some money and that I would be able to support my recently incurred expenses of the last few days.

I idled up to the empty spot at the unloading dock and tied up the boat. A voice yelled down asking, "Where can we put the large stainless steel unloading bucket?" There was little to no room on the deck of my boat so I suggested they lower it onto the small float beside the stern. That way I could lean over and place the fish into the tub quite easily. Those seven fish would not nearly fill the bucket, it would only be one trip up, but still it was better than a finger delivery. After I helped lower the tub into place, I jumped into the stern of my boat and made ready to transfer the fish over.

I grabbed the largest fish first and with two hands placed it into the bucket, and added the twenty-pounder next. I slid the last 5 fish onto my fingers in behind the gill flaps; the two springs in my right hand went in first followed by the last three in my left hand. As I was lifting the last three fish up I felt a rip in the gill area of one of the fish. The flap on that one tore away from the jaw and I watched in horror as it slid off my finger, fell between the boat and dock and began sinking into the water. I quickly tossed the other two into the bucket and grabbed my gaff. Grasping it I took a swing through the water but was too late. I watched over the side as the fish slowly drifted away from me, down deep and out of sight to the bottom. *Crab bait,* I thought. There were some smirks from the unloading crew over this and I can't say I blamed them. A finger delivery gone bad , so to speak, was not my idea of entertainment.

From that point on I made sure to clean all my fish properly, by not cutting the small piece of cartilage that joins the body to the lower jaw. Keeping the cartilage intact made the overall appearance of the fish better and was the way the buyers preferred the product to be delivered. This cleaning or dressing style was referred to as "princess dressed".

After unloading, I sheepishly slid ahead to make room for the next boat in line. There I used a high powered hose to wet everything down and with a bit of Sunlight dish soap added, I scrubbed my checkers until they were soon sparkling clean. I think I probably scrubbed extra hard that day as I tried to forget what had just happened with the lost fish. From then on, when delivering, I never attempted to put more than one fish in my hands. It would be one at a time only and it never happened again.

My fishing pattern remained unchanged for the next week. I alternated between the Duval Point and Masterman Island tacks. It was not big fishing but certainly enough came into the boat each day to keep me coming back for more. Mainly I caught springs but a few more Coho salmon started to show up as well. The larger ones could really shake the lines as they fought hard to get free. The bigger the fish, the better the price would be. At that time for Coho salmon we were paid a $1.25 a pound for fish three to five pounds, $1.50 for five to seven pounds and for any sizes over that $1.85 pound. I quickly learned that Coho salmon are aggressive feeders and that they'd often grab the top pieces of gear near the surface. I added a few more spoons and flashers to each of my four lines and this seemed to increase my overall production. They were definitely fun to catch.

"Frying Pan Dave"

Despite a steady scratch here I was beginning to feel it was time to try some new ground; the same scenery day after day can tend to get boring. The next chain of islands outside of Hardy Bay was called the Gordon Group and I thought it was time to give it a whirl. My chart clearly showed an edge that could be worked at the bottom end, with a small rock marking the most southern point of the reef. John periodically checked this spot but on this particular day, I was there alone. Fishing this ground was only a fifteen minute run, straight out from Duval Point, making it still very accessible for day fishing.

I dropped the lines in the deep, then slowly eased my way towards the edge. A couple of passes later I had, with eyes glued to the sounder, figured out most of the ins and outs of the tack. A quick glance at the shoreline gave me an outside visual of when shallow spots were nearing.

Landmarks can be a vitally important source of information. Fishermen who stayed exclusively in one small area or spot were often referred to as "homesteaders". They could virtually fish by landmarks alone, only occasionally having to look at their sounder.

Len and Marian on the *Starlite* would be in that category, Len pretty much fished the Jeanette Islands, a strong tidal area closer to the mainland shore, about two hours run from Port Hardy. This was "his spot" so to speak. Few other boats fished there and I believe Len and Marian liked the privacy better than fishing amongst a larger group of boats. Besides, it was a very short tack with not a lot of room for traffic. It was a common saying that Len could fish that tack with his eyes closed and I could believe it. This was not the case for me here at this new spot, however. The tide was running hard that day and I had to be extra aware and careful. With my gear in the water, I gradually moved closer in, looking for feed and the telltale seabirds that would at many times appear on the surface seemingly from nowhere. Where there was one type of bird there were usually others, cormorants being the most common. This part of the coast could be a banquet for the many different species of waterfowl, which often showed their catch in their bills when surfacing, be it an eel fish, herring or candlefish. They had a large selection of food to pick from.

The southernmost tip of this tack was marked by a small visible rock with another mostly submerged one right below it. The hidden rock was marked by a large kelp bed that came more clearly into view at low tide. This kelp acted as kind of a marker buoy and warned you of the rock's presence. The tide, when flooding, would want to push you on your stern quarter towards this hazard. You had to angle away from it in advance of that shallow edge. About the fourth time trolling by it that morning I ventured in a little too close. The flashing red signal rose sharply on the sounder screen and the boat started to list, I had snagged bottom and was really caught in its grip. The springs on the pole were stretched to their maximum, both the deep line and the pig on the starboard side. There was kind of a bang as the lead on the deep line let go, freeing that line, but the pig line was not moving. Looking back I could see the styrofoam float starting to sink under water. The boat started to list a little more and a feeling of panic ran through me as I quickly entered the wheelhouse to grab my wire cutters and take the boat out of gear. At this time the tag line at the end of the now bent pole parted, taking the strain off the pole but now the weight transferred itself directly to the block on the davit and also the gurdie. The tide was running hard and although I had put the brake on that spool, the line continued to slip and run slowly out. The lead did not release its grip. The strain was immense and I looked up to see the davit starting to bend. The davit was made of two inch steel pipe. I quickly cut the wire line and finally freed the boat. The ocean floor fell off quickly at the end of the rock so the boat and gear on the other side had managed to stay free from danger. I put the *Antique* back in gear and picked up what lines were left in the water and then quickly assessed the situation.

What a mess! Two of my leads were gone, one float had been lost and four pieces of gear from one line were history. I felt a little sick in the stomach. What made matters worse was that I had no extra leads and the day was still young.

In the meantime the float had resurfaced so I idled the *Antique* slowly up beside it, took her out of gear and then snagged the pig with my gaff. I unhooked it from the steel line then carefully let the rest go back in the water, being first sure it was all clear of the propeller. I did not need any more drama; I'd had enough for one day. Luckily I had retrieved something back; an important item, too, as I had no spare floats either.

I moved the boat out into deeper water and pondered the situation. It was too early in the day to go back in and here I was, down over fifty dollars from losses with no fish to show for it. To continue fishing I had to find some weight in order to get all the gear back to its proper depth. The boat trolled too fast for spring salmon especially; I needed the drag of all four lines in the water to slow it down enough. I rummaged through the boat's cupboards and under the bunk all I could find that might be heavy enough to do the trick was a large cast iron frying pan and a small steel bucket full of rusty old nuts and bolts. *It's worth a try*, I thought. *What do I have to lose?*

Back in the stern again, I re-spliced the steel lines, forming a loop on both ends, then I connected the frying pan to the deep line and attached the bucket of bolts to the pig line. Ready to go, I put the boat back in gear and doggedly returned to business. I lowered the bucket into the water first and then attached two pieces of gear, lowering the line to twenty fathoms. Then I put on the pig and floated her back behind the boat to a safe enough distance to clear the deep line. The float sat high in the water as there was not enough weight to pull it down to where it should be. Next went the frying pan into the depths and I watched as it moved back and forth like a flasher of some kind; it did not take long to realize this was not going to work. After one short tack I decided to pick up the gear. The bucket must have released its contents to the sea floor as the float was now lying flat on its side. My innovations had proven pointless.

I coiled up the gear and put everything back in place as if nothing had happened. *Not a good day*, I thought to myself and headed the boat back to port. An hour later I tied up to the fuel dock and prepared to go in and press further into my line of credit. I was not in a good mood. A few people came over to see what was up, being that I was in the harbour earlier than usual. "Need more leads," was all I said as I entered the store; Rick gave me a quizzical look as I moved over to the cannonball section.

I'd better stop trying to go cheap here and by more than one at a time, I thought. So I purchased two twenty-five pounders and two twenty pounders. I picked up one of the large steel hooks with its tee-handle and short shaft, then slipped the end of it through the eye on top of the lead. I carried them out to the *Antique*, with one in each hand.

By now there was a small crowd around the stern of my boat. My pal John was in the middle of the gathering, pointing and laughing. "That's a first!" he said, "A frying pan for a cannonball." *Great, just what I don't need right now*, I thought.

I kicked myself then for not thinking to hide the evidence better or at least disconnect it altogether before I docked. With all that had gone wrong that morning, I just did not think about it. Though it was partially hidden in the checkers it obviously was not covered well enough to escape John's sharp eye. He shook his at head at me. This was all a little embarrassing to say the least.

I had not much to say, but briefly told my side of the story. John added, "At least he tried to keep the gear in the water." Such ribbing, as always, was meant in good taste and looking at the situation facing me, I had to admit it was pretty funny. The last thing I needed, however, was to be centre stage over this. But for the rest of that season, whenever John and I shared a beer, the frying pan always had to come up. Of course, this tale got better each time depending on the audience. Near the end of the year people travelling south from Prince Rupert were heard asking "did you hear about the guy and his frying pan?" The tale had travelled up and down the coast. It haunted me for a very long time and to top it all off, I soon learned that I had earned a new nickname; I was no longer known as "Antique Dave" my new handle was "Frying Pan Dave."

I rarely fished the Gordon Group after that, not only because of that experience but whenever I did try it, I never caught anything. From that day onward and wherever I fished, I only ever tied a single loop of ganion twine to my leads so they would release easier and not "bring the house down" if I snagged bottom again. I guess in the beginning I did not want to give any gear up and I doubled up on everything. This way would now basically cut the release power in half. However, the slight permanent bend in my davit served as a constant reminder of that day and how it could have been so much worse.

It was not uncommon to see other boats with pole tips broken off or worse. Having to change a trolling pole in midseason could be time consuming and costly, but it was the price sometimes paid to "scratch fish" amongst the rocks. There was always the possibility of getting tangled up and this was a battle you seldom won.

Deserters

One day John asked me if I wanted to try out some new ground, and to that I enthusiastically responded, "Let's do it." He suggested the next chain of islands over, located in about the middle of Queen Charlotte Strait. They were aptly named The Deserter Group or more commonly "The Deserters". This chain of islands was about an hour and fifteen minutes from Port Hardy and about halfway between the Gordon Group and the Jeanette Islands. It would mean an overnight stay and that would be something new to me at this time. I had nothing to cook on so I bought a Coleman stove while in Port Hardy along with some extra food and a few necessary utensils. Of course, maybe now I could put my infamous frying pan to better use.

John picked up a little ice for his fish hold and soon we were ready to go. I was not equipped to pack any ice at that time. My tiny hold was used to carry only spare rope, extra motor oil and other vital things I might need. The *Antique* was a true day boat. We left early in the afternoon and I basically followed John from a safe distance behind. The water was flat calm when we set out; once past the Gordon Group, we then altered our compass course slightly to the north. We arrived a short time later and prepared to get our gear into the water. That gave me some time to familiarize myself with the grounds and to get a feel for the tack.

I watched John ahead of me, noting where he made his turns and I did the same. The actual tack was fairly short although there was enough shoreline depth to extend it if needed. There was a showing of feed, which is always a good sign, and I watched John land a nice spring but I did not get anything. We picked up our gear after a couple of hours. John would explain to me later this place is known for its morning bite. One usually did not catch much at all after four in the afternoon here; you wanted to be on the tack early at daylight. With the gear stowed away I followed close behind John again, heading for a narrow opening that is barely visible until you've actually entered it, and narrow it was.

From a distance you would never have seen this little channel, it blended in so well. But here it was, a place so tight you could not have squeezed through with your poles down. We stopped briefly and pulled our poles up into the crosstree, then eased the boat back into gear and idled along for about 100 yards; there were cliffs on both sides of us. Then suddenly the channel opened up to a small lagoon. The bottom was clearly visible all the way in, with a shallow rock on the left that had to be skirted around as you entered the more open area.

Taking any sizable boat in there could play on the nerves, but once in, you could anchor safely in the sandier bottom below. The best approach was to hug the starboard shore before it opened up; there it was the deepest, but even then it might only give five to six feet of depth at low tide. It really was not a place for larger vessels but we were fine with ours. The lagoon was about three hundred feet long overall.

The best part of it all, however, was the small tie-up area present, that meant you did not have to anchor. There was a large cedar log about four feet in diameter with a boom chain on either end of it where you could tie your lines to. This log was lashed by cable and bolted to two other logs at either end. These logs ran up into the bush where they were bolted to the base of two large stumps about forty feet apart. The big log could rise and fall with the tides as all the connections were done in such a way to allow for its movement. Someone had gone to a lot of trouble to set up this moorage arrangement and it was well constructed.

I waited for John to secure his boat, and then I tied up beside him. "This was not here last season," he commented. It was too isolated to be a private moorage, so we sat there for a while and took it all in. What a place. We found out later that the tie-up float had been put together by a fellow named Dave Hopkins. He and his wife, Wendy, owned a 38 foot troller called the *Lazy David*. They often frequented this special little place and earlier in that same year, they had put the whole thing together for all to use. Dave and Wendy, I learned, usually fished for pink salmon further north, in the central part of the coast. Later on that summer I would meet them in Port

Hardy as they were on their way south. I spotted their boat tied up at the Seafood's float and went over to say *Hi* and thank them for their great little innovation in this remote part of the coast. Their tie-up area certainly made The Deserters a more attractive place to fish, especially for me. Little did I know then that this would be my first of many nights here; I was about to become a "homesteader".

After shutting our engines off, John and I sat on our decks and had a beer together. It was so quiet. We talked about fishing; about John's past years on old halibut schooners and of some of our present day adventures. I did not have a lot to offer, being new, but I sure listened intensely to John's stories; he had so many good ones to tell. It was soon time to get dinner going and I started up my Coleman stove on the small hatch cover. I boiled up some potatoes to have along with a few pork chops and onions. John, who had an oil stove on his boat, was down below on the *R.W.* cooking up one of his favorite meals; short ribs with all the trimmings.

An oil stove, I thought. It seemed like such a luxury item to me at the time. We ate together in silence; the food was so good. After dinner I cleaned up my dishes, washing them over the side of the boat in the clear ocean water, and then got everything else ready for the morning. Daylight would arrive at around 4:00 o'clock here but with John, "morning" always seemed to come a little sooner. He liked a very early start and it was not uncommon for him to be up and about at 3:30 getting the coffee pot going.

I sat on my hatch cover after dark quietly taking it all in; I had this feeling of being so far away from anywhere. It was a perfectly clear night and the stars seemed to literally jump out at me; truly nature in all her glory. The only other light was the one that dimly shone from John's cabin, below decks. The anticipation of catching fish, maybe the big one, rested in my mind amidst all of this and I thought to myself, *How lucky am I to be here.* A short while later I turned in to my bunk and put an extra blanket over me. The night air was definitely a little cooler here. *It sure would be nice to have the oil stove one day*, I thought as I drifted off into a deep sleep.

I woke with a start to the sound of my alarm clock and climbed out of bed. After a big stretch, I climbed the two steps to the deck. It was still very dark but John's cabin light was glowing and he invited me in for coffee. He always had a jab for me and that morning he said, "It sure is warm in here, what a good sleep I had." I grinned at this but was too sleepy to respond. We always liked to share a laugh together, no matter where and no matter when. He was well aware, by now, of my little vessel's shortcomings.

As daylight started to appear I untied the *Antique* and followed John out of the comfort of the anchorage. We were the only two boats on the tack when I started putting the gear out in deeper water. With everything in place it was time to make a turn and start the tack up the beach. I set the gear at twenty fathoms and kept a steady eye on the sounder. The flashes on the sounder grew stronger as the bottom started to angle upward and at about thirty fathoms I straightened the rudder out, but the bottom continued to climb. Suddenly the flashes got very strong and I turned the wheel further to port and opened the throttle a little. I'd gone over a small, shallow spot but had managed to raise the leads up over it with a bit of speed. I idled back down, letting the lines I was dragging settle back to their normal depth. This I stored in my memory bank for the next time.

Once you were past this first point you would then angle sharply back in towards shore and then straighten out for about a hundred feet. This would take you close to the mouth of the anchorage and once that was in view you'd make a gentle turn and head back the other way. The whole tack from turn to turn was about five hundred yards long so it did not take long to troll up the edge. Depending on how many other boats were there you would generally troll down on the outside, in the deep, as the boat inside of you with its starboard pole toward the beach had the right of way.

This right of way agreement is a critical rule when trolling amongst the rocks as you had to give the boat inside of you room to turn out. Not doing so could cause loss of gear and hot tempers to follow. Over the years there has been more than one good yelling match back and forth between boats. Without this simple, but vital rule in place, things could be chaotic.

Being as only John and I were there, we both had lots of room. If you happened to be there by yourself, you could take the edge going both ways, but this was fine.

Trolling down the tack on the outside gave me a good chance to check the gear and I thought I had something on my starboard deep line. I brought the line-up and, sure enough, on the bottom piece of gear I had a small ling cod. It wasn't much, but it was worth something. I checked one of the back lines and came up with nothing, but this step was always worth taking.

Being sure that all the gear was clean would mean a better chance of catching what you were after, ideally a large spring; you just never knew when one would bite.

With both lines back in the water it was time for me to once again turn and head up the shore. I made a long, slow swoop and cut in about one hundred yards behind John. With my eyes on the sounder I adjusted the throttle a little and edged my boat in and out of the rock ledges twenty fathoms below. I glanced ahead to make sure I was not too close to John. I could see him in the stern of his boat fighting a fish. Just to be on the safe side, he had angled out a little farther from the edge. It takes a long time to learn how to do both; being able to watch where you're going and to keep focused on getting the fish into the boat. It seemed to come easily for John. *Maybe the bite was on*, I thought. It was getting close to the morning's tide change, a time when things were usually supposed to happen.

I glanced out the port window and noticed my deep line spring start to move in and out. Holding my breath with excitement I kept my eyes on the line making sure the fish had not broken free. I could see he was still on, as the tugging motion continued. Looking ahead I saw John still battling his fish. It must be big as this fight was taking a while. As he started to edge the fish closer to his boat I watched him reach for something in his cockpit, he then pointed it towards the water and I heard a sudden bang: it was a hand gun. The fish went still, and smoothly John flipped it aboard with his gaff. Even at this distance, it looked to be about a thirty pounder, a nice salmon. John would only use this technique on large fish that were tough to handle as it made it easier for him to get them on board. The idea was to shoot at the head area to stun the fish for the short moment it took to land them. Other fishermen also used this technique but you had to be careful as there were stories of the big ones that got away due to an errant shot that cut the line. Hitting a moving object in the right area can be tough.

I didn't carry a gun so I would usually, at the right moment, and when in position, hit the fish on the head with the back of my gaff. Then I'd quickly turn the gaff around and bring the fish into the boat with the hook end. Here again you had to be careful, a glancing blow, as I'd already found out, would only make a salmon angry and off they would run at full speed. At that point all you can do is watch anxiously, hoping the line does not break or the hook straighten out. It was 50/50 depending on the size of the fish; the big ones quite often would just keep on going.

Turning my attention away from John, I saw that my own fish was still on the line. With the combination of excitement and anticipation that always comes with these moments, I took my position in the stern of the boat. Like John, I stayed out from the edge a little so I could fully concentrate on the job ahead and not worry about the bottom below. The first piece of gear was slack and I coiled it into the boat and then did the same with the second piece. As the fish neared the surface, the main, steel line and cannonball started to move back and forth and away from the boat. The adrenaline rush that comes in this moment is really one of the things that keeps you in the game; this is what it is all about. It is hard to describe unless you have actually done it. But I can tell you now that through all the years of bringing in a big fish, the feeling and excitement that comes with it never fades.

I then reached down to the piece of gear that held my prize. The fish was on a long leader with a wonder spoon at the end as bait. The fish was straight out, off the side of the boat, jerking his head back and forth trying to shake free of the hook that held him. He was big, probably twenty-five pounds plus. I slowly tried to lead him in towards me which worked for about eight feet. At that point he decided to take a run in another direction. The slack line sped through my hand but went tight again as he made a wild dash straight off the stern of the boat; the line held. I grabbed the perlon again to regain control of the fish, then suddenly he came straight out of the water, trying to throw the hook. I kept the line tight this time and again tried to bring him closer to me. This time he came with less fight as he was beginning to tire.

I quickly looked ahead to make sure the boat was on its proper course, and then I got back to the business of getting him onboard. Even though tiring, the fish still stubbornly tried to pull away but not hard enough to gain ground. I got my gaff hook ready and in reach when it would be needed, then slowly hand over hand I pulled him closer to striking range. At about three feet from the boat I reached back and grabbed my gaff. I turned the hook upwards, making ready to try and stun him with the back edge first, before pulling him aboard. He stared at me and I stared at him. The fish was in just the right position, lying in the water on his side, and in one more foot he would be close enough. Don't lose him, I nervously thought. I guided him a little bit closer, then raised the gaff and swung down to hit the fish on top of the head. I misjudged a little and the wooden club instead glanced off the side of his nose. That did it, he went nuts and the line sped quickly out from my hand, tightening for a moment, and then went slack. He had broken free; my worst fear came true. It was as if I'd talked myself into this happening; I had a feeling I was going to lose him and I did. I would eventually realize that the power of positive thinking was a big part of the fishing game.

For now, however, I could only feel anger with myself. Gone, another piece of gear, my new five and a half wonder spoon, in a lost battle. All I had to show for it was another story for the dock, if that. As the gear went back into the water I couldn't erase from my thoughts what had just happened. How big was it? Probably close to a thirty pound fish, in other words a $75.00 dollar bill. I had to shake it off and concentrate on the business at hand; *Maybe there's even a bigger one down there,* I mused. I gradually eased my way back onto the tack and over the next couple of hours landed four fish: two Coho and two springs. The springs were about eighteen to twenty pounds each and they definitely helped to spruce up the day, and my mood.

Around 1:00 o'clock John picked up his gear and headed back to Port Hardy and a couple of tacks later, after no action, I did the same. Once my gear was on board I stopped to pick up a couple of pieces of kelp that were floating by. These I placed over the top of my cleaned fish to keep the skin from drying out in the air. I then threw a bucket of seawater over all for good measure; again it was John who offered this little tip to me.

I arrived at the Seafood's unloading dock and was in line to deliver right after John. Tying up I went over to chat. He had seven nice springs for his morning effort; not a bad pay check. Of course my side of the discussion had to include the one that got away. John laughed and assured me that it would not be the last time that would happen and he was right, it wasn't. All in all, though, it was a great fishing experience and I had been introduced to a spot that I really liked.

John suggested we go to dinner that night at a very popular local restaurant in Port Hardy, Mae's Café. "If you want a really good homemade meal this is where you come," he told me, "It's a very popular place among the fishermen and it's usually full." It turned out to be quite small but cozy, having only about ten tables with four chairs at each. John knew most of the people there that night and I said *Hi* to a few that I recognized. Mae owned the place and she came over to our table right away. She was a short, petite Chinese woman whose warm smile made you feel right at home. She took our order and, being renowned for their steak, we both ordered: the T-bone dinner. John knew what to expect and when the food arrived I must say I was not disappointed. The large plate was full, with the steak taking up half the plate; what space remained was filled with mashed potatoes and gravy with peas on the side. You never left Mae's hungry and it was very affordable. Throughout that season I would eat there about once a week. It was a welcome relief to my cooking and the usual, predictable meals.

Lesson Learned

Time was moving on. It was now the second week of July and every day seemed to grow

coho wobbler

more important. Peak fishing periods were starting and I was hoping I'd have the opportunity to start banking a little more money. But there were rumors of the shore workers going on strike, and this concern only added more pressure to everything. I now had four tacks out of the Hardy Bay area that I could fish, but spent most of my time trying my luck at The Deserters. One day, I was routinely fishing the spot by myself. John was scratching away at the Gordon Group not more than fifteen minutes away; there did not seem to be enough fish for two boats to share, at either place. The tides were getting bigger as we were nearing the full moon and this also did not seem to help our production.

I had made a turn at the bottom of the now familiar tack and started to head up the beach. I thought I had seen a bite on my starboard pig line and, not wanting to wait, pulled the line in to check it. I was seemingly more impatient that day; slow fishing can do that to you. The pig was lying on a slight angle created by the force of the stronger tides. I continued to pull it in towards the boat, only to have it tangle with my deep line. This was not good and usually resulted in lost gear. I angled the boat slightly off the beach and put the break on the pig line gurdie, then I engaged the main line. It struggled under the weight of the two lines. The pig now lay on its side as the weight was taken up by the top piece of gear on the main line, a green Coho wobbler. It was amazing the perlon did not break under the strain. There it was, stubbornly supporting forty-five pounds of lead being dragged through the water by the force of the moving boat. Not wanting to lose the wobbler by cutting it, I grabbed the edge of the hook between the finger and thumb of my left hand; it was really tight. I pulled the hook back until it released its tight grip on the steel line then let the wobbler go. Instead of shooting back into the water the hook tore directly into the flesh at the base of my middle finger, barely missing the bone, and coming out the other side. Blood started oozing freely from the wound. The force had pulled me square to the stern and bent me slightly over. I stared into the water, I was totally trapped, attached by the hook to the line in the water. I felt a small wave of panic and looked around for my knife. It was not there. Then off to the side of the landing box, I spotted it, just out of my reach.

To make matters worse, with all the extra drag on one side, the boat wanted to head in the direction of shore. Fortunately I was able to steer the *Antique* with my right knee and angle it so it was somewhat off the beach; this helped a little. I couldn't believe the small amount of muscle in my middle finger was holding all this weight. What could I do? I thought for a moment and then, taking a deep breath, I grabbed the perlon with my right hand and took a single wrap on it. Having a good grip on it now, I pulled hard on the line, taking the strain off my bleeding finger, and gained a couple of feet. I then quickly placed my left knee on the perlon, and this freed up my right hand for an instant. Turning my body I was barely able to reach my knife with that hand, but managed to and then with a quick slash I cut the perlon, freeing me from my dilemma. There was no pain for the moment but things were a mess.

By now, John had moved over to where I was, to give it a try himself. Upon arriving he soon realized that something was wrong. As quickly as possible, I stowed all my gear on board, despite the blood, and with the Coho wobbler hanging from my left hand. John idled up close beside me and with a quick look he pretty well summed up the situation. "All you can do is cut off the barbed end and pull it through," he called over to me. This I did, with my rusty wire cutters. "You will have to go into Port Hardy to the clinic and get a tetanus shot," he added. I poured some Dettol on the wound to clean it and wrapped it tightly with a paper towel. The bleeding seemed to stop somewhat but now came the throbbing.

Nodding in thanks to John for his advice, I headed the *Antique* towards Hardy Bay, reflecting on how lucky I'd been, once again. *It could have been worse*, I told myself. And all of this happened because I wanted to save a twenty-five cent spoon. Back in Port Hardy I tied the boat up to the government wharf and headed up town to the clinic where I had everything looked after.

It would be the only and last time I ever did that. Whenever I'd have a similar tangle in the future, I'd grab the hook with a pair of pliers, and either cut the line to save the piece of gear or just let it go. From that day on, my knife and wire cutters were always accessible in the stern; it was a lesson learned.

Fog

At this time of year there was a constant stream of boats moving in and out of Port Hardy as more and more fish openings occurred for the net fleet, especially in the central and northern parts of the coast. We, as trollers, were not affected as much; it was business as usual, being open seven days a week. The only significant change was it made for was a busier place. Often you had to put your name on a waiting list to deliver your fish, as many boats could already be lined up ahead of you. These line ups were especially long after a seine and gillnet opening. They would start on Sunday at 6pm and run steadily for two to four days, depending on the amount of fish in any given area. You had to be especially alert at all times especially when fishing Duval Point. It was a main travel route for boats coming and going. This situation could be further complicated by a curve ball Mother Nature can throw at you this time of year, that being fog.

Fog was quite common here, especially from late July through until the end of August and into early September. It was caused when the cooler ocean temperatures collided with the warm summer air and when there was no wind the fog could settle in thick for days on end; at times it would persist even with a breeze.

It did not create too big of a problem if you had a little item called "radar" but of course the *Antique* did not have this feature. A brand new radar system then cost about $4500, and that was almost what I'd paid for the boat. The Japanese-based marine electronics company that manufactured the radar units,

Furuno, had a lease-to-purchase program but it was still too much money for me at the time. Coming up with a down payment would have been a real struggle.

John had a radar unit on his boat and when fog became an issue I would follow close behind him to Duval Point or Masterman Island where I could at least get the gear in the water. Unfortunately both these places had the most boat traffic, but being close to the beach there when trolling, I could usually make out the black rocks of the shore through the fog. However, coming from within the mist, there seemed to be a constant swell and steady hum of boats moving by outside of me. Often this would be the only evidence that they were present; the fog visually swallowed them up. It was all very stressful and at times I would have to follow the shoreline back to Hardy Bay. Seeing land as I idled along the beach gave me a sense of security, but there were times even then when I would lose sight of land; it could be that thick. In especially heavy fog, I would find myself once in a while following closely behind a passing vessel so I could get back to the safety of the dock.

Fog can play tricks on your eyes. Sometimes you would think you saw a shadow of something that wasn't there; it could tug at your mind. A low flying cormorant or a small flock of sea birds could appear suddenly and then be gone in a split second. I'd often jump at these times, and my nerves would be strained further. As the end of July neared the fog remained a constant challenge. On days of a more cloudy nature, when the wind was from the south, the air seemed a little cooler and fog was not usually a problem. However, when the sun was out due to a more north westerly weather pattern, fog could be present.

Picking my days, I scratched away at Duval Point and Masterman Island, but I was anxious to get back to the Deserter Group. Spring salmon runs heading for the Nimkish River, Knights and Kingcome Inlets would be building at this time of year and this was probably a good time to be there.

One morning I awoke to blue skies. From Hardy Bay it was clear to the Gordon Group where, like a line had been drawn, the fog started. It was, however, a low lying fog as you could see the mountains on the mainland shore in behind, but not the water. The fog bank seemed to be seventy feet high and above that the air was totally clear. *How bad could that be?* I thought, *It will probably clear up.* And so I set off from Hardy Bay with The Deserters as my destination. All was fine, no wind, and a beautiful clear day until I rounded the bottom end of the Gordon Group, then suddenly I was enveloped by fog. Being under the illusion that there wasn't real cause for concern had been a mistake and it did not take too long for my "not that bad" mindset to disperse.

Upon entering the fog bank, the mist was thin and I could see a short distance ahead and behind. But it quickly got worse and thickened as I moved along. Yet when I looked up there was blue sky. It was the strangest thing. Relying on my compass only, I stubbornly moved on as I knew the course that would lead me to my destination. Looking ahead I could hardly see the bow of my little vessel. Then over the sound of my motor, I suddenly heard a distant blast from a horn that came from somewhere off my starboard side. *There are no light houses in this general area,* I thought to myself, *It has to be a boat.*

I was now nearing the middle of Queen Charlotte Strait,

which is an open stretch of water frequented by very large ocean-going vessels heading either up or down the coast; it was their preferred route. I went outside the cabin to better listen over the constant drone of my diesel engine and the horn sounded again, warning others of its presence. It definitely came from east of me and, back at the steering wheel, I idled the motor down. This cut back my speed but also reduced the engine noise so I could better hear. Again the horn sounded and this time it was louder. I took the *Antique* out of gear, then went outside on deck and closed the door behind me. The air was very still. My eyes strained and my ears listened intently but there was not a sound. I felt a knot slowly growing in my stomach. Suddenly there was a louder blast; whatever it was sounded very close.

There are times in a person's life when you become totally gripped by fear and this was one of my moments. They are often referred to as "having your heart in your throat," and mine was. It was then that I thought I could hear something; a faint rumbling sound broke the silence, adding further to my inner panic. Suddenly, another loud blast seemed to come from directly in front of me and the deep rumbling grew louder. I stood there frozen, my eyes straining to detect movement of any kind and it was then that I saw it. Probably no further than two hundred yards away, the upper deck of a cruise ship went past, blocking out much of the blue sky above. Lifeboats and the huge exhaust stacks were all I could see. The rest of the massive vessel was hidden in the fog. As quickly as it appeared, it was gone. Moving at twenty knots, it was swallowed back up by the fog in seconds.

As if in a bad dream and like nothing had just happened, I eased my boat back into gear and then turned to idle into the large swells that would inevitably be arriving from its stern. After about five minutes of bobbing up and down and when the sea once again was calm, I turned the *Antique* around and headed back to port. It did not take long before I emerged from this foggy nightmare. The sun shone down and it was clear sky all around me once again. Looking through the wheelhouse window ahead I thought I saw a flash of something in my reflection and, no, I do not think I was imagining this, it was my first grey hair.

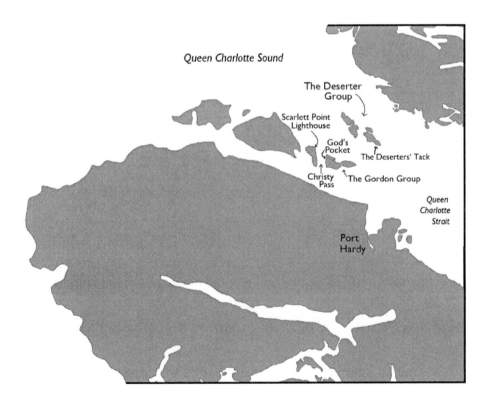

Sometime near the end of July, 1975, a strike vote was taken by the shore workers, tender men and cannery workers. All were in favour of striking. Within a couple of days all delivery plants would close; us fishermen would have only that short period of time to come in and deliver any fish we had onboard. This was not good; the peak times were here as sockeye and pinks were on their way to spawning grounds nearby and further south of here. That is, of course, why the industry would strike now, thereby exerting more pressure for a quick settlement. The U.F.A.W.U (United Fishermen and Allied Workers Union) and The Native Brotherhood requested that all fishermen cooperate and support their cause. Although I was not a member of the union it did not matter; as fishermen, we did just that.

All operations on shore would cease, and there would be nowhere to sell fish anyway so by sticking together, we all hoped for a quicker end to the strike. However, the rumors that came back to many of us then were not good. The demands being made were substantial and the strike could go on for a while. The harbour was soon jammed with many vessels tied to the docks. Some commuted home from Port Hardy, others, like me, stayed; the boat was my home.

Logging was shut down during fire season and to make matters worse for the Port Hardy community, Utah Mines, a large local employer was also on strike. There were a lot of disgruntled people. The pubs in the area were full and at 11o'clock opening time, the Seagate Hotel already had a large line-up outside waiting to get in. The stories and the talk grew louder as the day wore on and the more beer consumed the worse things could appear. With all the workers from different industries packed into the same place, it was obvious that there were bound to be many different opinions. Not everyone was in agreement with each other. Tensions would mount, and every once and awhile a fight would break out. It could be a zoo, so to speak, but more often than not it wasn't too bad.

Despite everyone being on edge, most of the time things were kept light and funny. I remember a Japanese fisherman by the name of Uki. He and his wife, Marge, would base out of Port Hardy during the summer months on their 38-foot troller. At the time I figured him to be a fit late forty's or early fifty's; I can still see him doing a hand stand on one of the small oval bar tables, then doing a series of arm push ups from there. It was a great show and brought smiles and cheering from all around. Of course there was lots of arm wrestling and other fairly harmless things going on as well.

I usually sat with many of the different fishermen I had come to know. John, Paul and others were good, familiar company and I would listen to their conversations, offering what I could. Paul was very vocal about what was going on and seemed to know a lot about the situation. A smart man, he could draw conclusions and compare the problem of the day to those that had happened in the past, and not only in the fishing industry. Paul was kind of a historian. At times he would lose me in the conversation, and when he did he always seemed to sense it. When he had a point to make, he wanted your full attention. If he did not have it he would tap me or whomever on the shoulder and then raise both arms straight up in the air continuing to talk in this fashion. It didn't matter if either one of you were sitting or standing.

Paul was about 6'3" with dark eyes, a full graying beard and an always present fishing hat. He was a presence and whenever he would do this, you listened. I forget who first gave him the nickname, but because of his habit he was affectionately referred to as "Trolling Poles Paul".

I tried to keep my own conversations light as I was vague on the politics and details of this current situation. I guess the bottom line was we were all in the same boat; no fish meant no money coming in and not many were very happy with this scenario.

The bar scene, I realized after a few days, was not the place to frequent. I could not afford it for starters and it became too repetitious, the same stories kept surfacing time and time again. There were a large group of people who had not gone home and they remained patiently waiting on their vessels all throughout Hardy Bay. It was especially crowded where I was tied up at the inner government dock. In places we were moored four abreast, it was jammed tight. I met people from all over, in particular a group from Courtenay, who were fun to be with. There was Bob on the *Nansen*, Dave and Joan on the *Kathleen* and several others I got to know. All we could really do was band together and ride it out.

One of the busier people that I met during this time was a fellow by the name of Joe Gillis, or "Reverend Joe", as the fishermen most commonly referred to him. He was in the marine electronics business working mainly in the repair end of things, as well as installing new equipment. So many of the vessels in port seemed in constant need of attention as far as electronic issues went, and Joe was in demand. My own boat had only a sounder on board, so I was not one of his regular clients. But many of the other boats of course had much more sophisticated equipment, therefore a greater need for repairs. As well as sounders, there were radio phones, including CB's, VHF, and single sidebands for long distance transmissions. There were also radars, sonars, auto pilots and lorans (long range navigation systems), especially common in the more offshore vessels. So there was lots of equipment to be maintained, with Joe being one of the guys that looked after the fleet in this regard.

Joe had a great sense of humor. He was tall, with curly light brown hair and a laugh that was infectious. If he laughed at something, whether you found it funny or not, it would bring a smile to your face. At times you would not see what boat he was working on, but you could hear him. The electronic items he serviced could be expensive and very dear to the people who owned them. Joe would set to work, get the cover off something, say the radar, undo a couple of wires, then lick his fingertip. He would then touch a wire and say, "Yep that's the hot one!"

Joe loved to have fun in his work. Regardless of his jovial manner, though, he was good at what he did and serious about the jobs he carried out. Some of his regular customers would take Joe to dinner or out for a beer when he had finished with their boat. It was not uncommon to see him in one of the local establishments. He was working long hours then and needed a break once in a while. When someone approached him he would occasionally say, "Yes my son?" He'd often say this before you had a chance to utter your first words, hence the name "Reverend Joe".

As I got to know him I came to realize that there was not a mean bone in Joe's body. It was always a treat to share a laugh with him as everything seemed to have a funny side; basically it was hard not to like the guy. On top of it all, he was straight up with his work and told you if something was worth fixing or not. With this honest approach, along with everything else, it was no wonder Joe was so popular with the fleet. And besides, especially during this period of time, a person could always use a good laugh now and then; something he often provided.

The strike lasted approximately three weeks, much longer than anyone wanted or expected. As it neared the end, it became clear that it had taken a toll on most of us. It had proved to be very draining both financially and otherwise. I joined the steady stream of boats that left the harbour shortly thereafter and went back to The Deserters.

Homeward Bound

For the next two weeks I fished the area steadily but things really didn't pick up or get any better; a lot of fish had already gone through by then. Many spring salmon were nearing the river mouths where they were born, waiting for the fall rain that would send them upstream to renew their cycle of life.

I began feeling a little homesick for Lund, not surprisingly, so early in September, I made plans to start the trip back south. Before leaving, I settled up my account, paying off what I had charged up over the season, and receiving a cheque for what was left. My gross so far that year was $3,500 and my take home was roughly around $1000 dollars. I'd not made a lot of money, but that did not depress or deter me. It did not seem to matter as much to me back then, the money part that is, because I was living my dream. I was young and driven, but best of all, loved what I was doing. It is hard to put a dollar value on that.

I left the next day and my trip back to Lund was safe and uneventful. I arrived two days later, in the early afternoon. As always, it was hard to come and go in Lund without being noticed and, sure enough, some people came down to the float to see me, curious to hear how my season had gone. It was a nice welcome home. After securing the boat and shutting everything off, I headed up the ramp with the others and entered the pub to have a beer. Art, Milly and Henry had just sat down and I walked over to join them. There were many hello's and handshakes and it seemed the atmosphere in the Lund bar had not changed, it was just like it had been when I left. It felt good to be back and, after ordering drinks for everyone, I reached into my pocket, pulled out a twenty dollar bill and handed it to Art. I thanked him again for his help and told the story of how his nice gesture helped to carry me north. We talked and talked, it was good to see and hear from everyone and get caught up on what had happened in Lund during the three months I'd been gone.

Chris and Diana came down to the pub and we shared a few light moments over a couple of drinks together. Later we walked back to their place and had a huge home cooked meal. Dinner parties here were a lot of fun and it was rather late when I arrived back at the *Antique* and crawled into my bunk. Needless to say, I missed the morning bite but it was good to have the day off, regardless.

Fishing around the Lund area, I learned, had not really picked up at all while I was away. Percy, a local Lund fisherman, decided to come over for a visit and have a talk about, you know, fishing. Percy lived in Finn Bay with a lady named Adrian, who just happened to be Henry's niece. He couldn't wait to give me a hard time about the "frying pan" story, which by now had also made its way down the coast; anything for a morning laugh. Percy was well known for being a good cod fisherman and he would often say "Anyone can catch a salmon but it takes a real fisherman to catch a cod." It was funny, him saying that, because I believe I had heard that same statement before from Henry. Obviously it was a common feeling amongst their families.

Percy had a 38-foot boat called *Elmi* and suggested I should try Stuart Island for spring salmon at this time of year. He told me he was heading there the next day to have a look at it himself. I did not know anything about the place as far as fishing went but Percy did. "In the early fall, apparently it can be good," he said. *Why not give it a whirl*, I thought. It was only four hours north of Lund, in what had by now become a somewhat familiar stretch of water for me. There would be lots of tide to deal with of course, and I'd basically only be able to fish slack water. Percy offered to pack my fish in his chilled hold as there'd be no buyers in that area and it would be too far to commute daily from Lund. "Plan to be there for roughly four to five days," he told me and so I grubbed up in the local store and made the boat ready to leave the following day. It was kind of like starting the season all over again as I idled out of the harbour the next morning. Pointing the bow north we passed by the Ragged Islands; the ocean was calm and a good day for travelling. I followed at a fair distance behind Percy, his boat being a couple of miles ahead on the horizon.

I arrived four hours later and tied up at the small float in front of the Stuart Island Lodge. Rob and Chris Kelly were there on the *Comet* along with a few other boats. They all had the same idea as us hoping to catch a few fall spring salmon to close out the season. The lodge seemed very quiet at that time of year and we talked to the owner about being able to moor there for a while. He was quite friendly and didn't mind us using his dock facilities at this time of year as things were quiet. Regardless of his generosity, we all chipped in a little money for him each day in exchange for that privilege.

There was a fuel dock located on a smaller finger beside where we were tied up and above that, up from the water there was a small store with a post office inside. To one side was another building, with large windows for better viewing; this was the lounge/restaurant area. It was a nice set-up and we supported this small business as much as we could afford to. South of this main building were eight or nine small separate guest cabins dotting the shoreline that housed the people who came here for sport fishing. The Stuart Island Lodge, in its surrounding little bay, was a very beautiful and picturesque place.

Percy and I had arrived shortly after slack water and therefore would have to wait for the next tide change to go fishing. Because of the strong currents in the area, you could only fish one hour before and one hour after slack water. Talking to the other fishermen tied up there, I got a good perspective on what to do. You'd set your gear at forty-five fathoms, which was quite deep for what I was used to. And you'd only fish one deep line on each side of the boat with just two flashers per line. It was too risky to fish with your pig lines at the back, these strong currents only increased the risk of tangles.

When it finally came time to leave the dock, the boats staggered themselves, one after the other, being sure to give each other lots of room. Usually the procedure here was to idle down current then turn and head upstream before putting out the gear. Once in place, we could troll our way up the edge of the short tack. We had to be careful not to troll too far up into the narrows as there was a shallow edge which stuck out from that point. If you were not watching closely it could easily strip you of your gear.

It was my turn to head out and I untied the *Antique,* heading her out into the swirling water. It was only minutes before I hit the drop-off and the point where I could start letting out gear. I drifted past the other boats and then turned my boat back into the tide. Looking at the beach I could see that I had already drifted down stream two hundred yards from where I had started; the tide was still running quite strongly.

Slowly I dumped out the gear and put the four flashers down to their proper depth. I then entered the wheelhouse to check the sounder as it was flashing a lot of red dots. I adjusted the gain to get a clearer reading of the bottom but it did not seem to change. There was lots of feed here but also the swirling currents made for a harder time getting a clear view of the bottom. The air bubbles in the water could create interference with the sounder image. I also had to keep a steady hand on the wheel as the tide wanted to push the boat around. I looked out and thought I had seen a tug at the end of my one pole. Within a minute I was on it and sure enough, I brought in two nice springs; nine and twelve pounds respectively. *Wow! This is easy,* I thought.

Things were going along nicely, the tide was easing off as it neared slack and I made my turn, heading back up the tack. I landed a couple more fish and as I lowered the gear back to its proper depth I glanced in the wheelhouse to check the sounder. There appeared to be a lot more flashes, indicating either feed or bottom. I entered the cabin to have a closer look and it did seem the boat was quickly getting closer to the shallow reef. So I angled the bow sharply out off of the edge, but it was too late. The starboard deep line hung up and I hoped the lead would lose its grip with the bottom but it did not. The spring on the pole stretched to its maximum and the pole bent slightly, before the line parted half way up.

There were a couple of places where the old steel line had frayed a little due to the wear and tear of the long season. This was common at this time of the year, but if a line was too badly worn, it should be cut and spliced. Because it hadn't been attended to, now instead of only losing just the lead, I lost two pieces of gear and about twenty fathoms of line. The port side stayed clear of the edge and I kept it fishing while I worked on the other side. I had to add more steel line first before attaching a cannonball and two new flashers to it. All of this took time and I stayed clear of the edge until I'd made these necessary repairs. In about fifteen minutes I was back in business.

I checked the port deep line and was surprised to find a nice fourteen pound spring on the bottom flasher. Bonus! This took some of the sting out of the day's expenses. The tide was now slack but only for about half an hour, then it would start to run from the other direction. This is prime time for the bite to start and, looking at the other boats around me, there was evidence of fish being landed. All of a sudden both my lines started to go. With one glance at my sounder to get my bearings, I was out in the stern. Let the fun begin.

I pulled two nice eight to twelve pound springs off one side and a six pounder off the other; I now had seven fish. The sounder showed lots of red blips again, however this time it was feed, but it still made me jump a little after what had just happened earlier. I decided to make a sharp turn inside at this point as there was room to do so without cutting in front of anyone. The fish seemed to be milling around that bit of feed and I was hungry for more action. A quick turn like that meant I had to cut the boat in a smaller radius but with only two lines out I figured it would be easier to do. However the edge again started to come up quickly; I opened the throttle a little, but it was too late. Now my port line grabbed the bottom and the spring stretched till one side of it broke away from the pole.

I'd tried to get aggressive and it had cost me. The end result of that gamble was the same as before; the line eventually parted, only this time, just above the lead. The old, worn steel wire was now weaker in places than the ganion twine used to join this line to the cannonball. I now had some extra work to do once back at the dock but a larger concern was now looming as I brought in the line and its tangled gear. I quickly formed a new loop in the steel line at the base, spliced it and then attached my very last lead to it.

After I put new leader line on the two flashers, I lowered everything back down and I was in business again. I had managed to keep the boat pretty much on the tack, and a quick check of my starboard line, produced two more nice sized springs. They were not really big fish but still they would add up. I trolled through slack water and when the tide started to ebb, I landed five more small to medium fish in the next hour. I took a not-quite-so-aggressive approach, staying off of the edge a little bit. I could not afford to lose any more gear at this point as the boat's trolling speed would be way too fast if I only had one line in the water, even going against the tide.

I now had maybe time for one more tack, and a sense of urgency came over me, realizing this. I went about my business fluidly but quickly. I pulled another twelve pound spring aboard and then decided to free-wheel the gear back down. With this technique, and time being short, maybe I could grab one more fish before heading in. I had used this method before when in a hurry: you would ease the brake on your gurdie so the lead would take the line down by free falling. You had to be careful to not let it go too fast as the flashers could tangle. I snapped on the first flasher then missed one mark before putting on the second. Then I eased the gurdie handle back to take it out of gear and the lead started to free wheel down through the water. I could control the speed by easing gently back on the handle and everything should be fine. However the line started to rapidly gain speed and easing the handle back did little to slow it down enough. The lever seemed to stick, probably due to lack of lubrication. Now the wire was really flying off the spool and, panicking, I pulled back harder on the handle. The brake then decided to grab.

So much weight going out at high speed and too sudden of a stop would not lead to a good ending. There was kind of a bang as the force of the lead breaking free jolted the davit, and the cannonball kept right on going. Looking back, the forty-five fathoms of trolling wire rose up and floated behind me on the surface of the water. "Mad" was not the word. My last lead was now gone and what a pointless way to lose it. I pulled the tangled mess of gear back on board, then picked up the poles. At least I'd managed to get most of the gear back, all except the lead, of course.

After tying up to the dock I had a better opportunity to assess the situation. *No more leads, great, what am I going to do now*, I thought. I remember eyeing up the rocks on the beach at this point but a 25 pound rock is big and for sure not an option; it would have been a worse idea than the frying pan. *First things first,* I told myself and set to work cleaning my fish. It had not been a bad day in that department. Once done the rest of the boats were now in and I shared my dilemma with Percy. Fortunately he had plenty of extra leads on board and I decided to trade him seven fish for the equivalent value in cannonballs. That solved the problem for now.

I fished out of Stuart Island for another five days, and although the fishing dropped off somewhat, it still made for a pretty good end to that season. We could fish usually two tides in a day, and with them being smaller at this stage of the moon, it was not too bad. I am sure I would not want to be there when they were at their peak as your actual fishing time would have been drastically reduced. The tides were starting to build again and my loaf of bread was getting low. With the last day there yielding only two spring salmon; it was time to head back to Lund. My fish were stowed away in the hold of Percy's boat, iced down and ready to sell. I had time to reflect a little as we headed back home and thought of what improvements could be done to the *Antique* prior to the next year. There was by now, a growing list.

The springs on my trolling poles needed to be replaced; they were old and rusty and stretched out of proportion. On the dock at Stuart Island I managed to reattach the one that had broken away with a hose clamp but having the opportunity to look at them close up, I could see all of them were in need of repair. Although the poles had fortunately not broken during the course of the year, it was apparent that they were old and getting brittle; replacing them had to be put on the list as well.

Fishing at Stuart Island and at the Deserters had made me aware of the need to pack a little ice. It would allow me more freedom to fish longer and expand my horizons. I probably wouldn't have the room in that small hold to pack very much but it would free me from having to sell daily. It would be a luxury to sell my catch every second day and further help to avoid long lineups when delivering.

"Let's see, I could use a CB radio and the oil stove down below would be nice for heat and for cooking." The list could go on and on. Some of these items were expensive, however, and at this point out of my reach. There were some improvements that were affordable, though, and those I could work on over the course of the off season. The four hour trip back to Lund seemed to fly by and before I knew it I had securely moored the *Antique* to the government float. My first salmon fishing season was officially over.

3

The boardwalk at Lund Harbour.

Winter in Lund

It was late September and by now most of the fish were in front of their river mouths, waiting for that first rain so they could start the journey upstream to renew their cycle. Some, however, were still making the migration to their final destination as the timeframe of their arrival depended on which run and river they were heading to. Salmon spawn primarily from September through to December. Mother Nature has a way of staggering the salmon runs so not all fish go upstream at the same time. Pink salmon, for example, can migrate up a particular river, say, in August and a run of Coho can follow through sometime in October.

Fish on their way to the spawning grounds lose their appetite somewhat, eating sparingly. They were not as likely to take any gear a troller would offer, so much of the fishing that carried on in the fall was done by the "net fleet", that being seiners and gillnetters. These boats could be very abundant depending on several factors: what area would open, for how long, and of course the size and strength of the salmon run. The Department of Fisheries and Oceans determines how much should be taken, closing areas when they felt enough had been caught. This allows an adequate number of fish to reach the spawning grounds, thereby securing the future of the stock.

Henry's boat the *Pair a Dice* could gillnet as well as troll. He was good at both but enjoyed fishing in the fall with his gillnet, as it could mean big catches, depending on where you were. For me, though, I had neither the boat nor the finances to set up the *Antique* for gillnetting, especially being my first year. She was a gulf troller primarily and at this point, I was content doing just that.

Fishing, like so many other things in life, is a frame of mind. In my first full season I had already learned a bit about this; my confidence, especially, had grown. Henry and Art often would talk to me about this concept; basically, if you thought you were going to catch fish, you usually did. This knowledge was something I stored away for now, but I do remember Henry telling me once, "You never stop learning; the ocean, it seems, can show you something new every day." He was right.

The year, though not big, would carry me financially for only a short while. There were, of course, tales of big fishing on the "west coast" of the island and up north. Many of these places were more *open* and waters too rough for me to get to in the *Antique*. However, I came to realize that some of these stories were a little stretched or exaggerated but I was somewhat gullible then, and prone to believe a lot people told me. Fishermen are notorious for their stories, even if all they brought on now and again was a good laugh. Of course the longer in the tooth the fisherman, the more he had to tell and the better they could get. So, at times, it was necessary to filter through what was true and what was, for lack of a better word, "bullshit". Being the newcomer, my stories were limited, although I admit that, yes, the twenty-five pound spring did grow to become a thirty-five pounder now and again. These tales were usually completely harmless and more often than not made for a more entertaining evening over a glass of beer.

It seemed now I had more time to reflect on my first year as a west coast fisherman. First off, I had bought a boat without having any previous fishing experience or knowing much of anything about the sea; basically learning as I went along. Combined with a slow start to the season and a strike at the peak time, it definitely made for a below average kind of year. Yet, I still managed to come out feeling good about it all, despite clearing only a thousand dollars; well, of course, one thousand dollars did go a lot further back then, but still it wasn't a lot.

Regardless, Chris, along with a few other locals, decided they wanted to buy their own boats for the following season and make a start in this "lucrative" business. I decided to go with Chris and together we went from town to town, walking the docks and looking for the right boat at the right price. Buying a boat of any kind rarely happens in short order; I was an exception. Like buying a car, it can carry on for a long while, but for Chris it didn't take too long. A few weeks later he found what he was looking for in Vancouver and after getting his finances in place motored into Lund with his first troller, the *Neptune*. He could fish salmon with the boat for two more seasons before the "B" licence would expire; much like the *Antique*, it was a start. The *Neptune* was also a double ender, similar in style to the *Antique* and overall a good vessel. But being a foot shorter than mine, I took the opportunity to jokingly tease him about it; I had the "bigger boat".

By the middle of October, and thanks to Art, I landed a job working in the woods with him. The site was about 4 miles out of Lund on the gravel road that led to Okeover Inlet. The turnoff was marked by a small sign and our job was to widen the road somewhat by keeping the over-growth from taking over. There was roughly three months of work there and something I really needed financially.

Art and Milly's waterfront cabin was a short walk from my boat, easily reachable by the boardwalk surrounding the small cove. Milly would always offer me a coffee and once in a while I'd join them in a bacon and egg breakfast. This place was also home to Henry and often our conversation revolved around fishing. They treated me like family and their house always felt like my home away from home. At around 7:30 Art and I would walk up to where he parked his truck and head off to the job site in order to start work by 8:00 a.m.

Clearing brush to widen the road was a good job and, with just the two of us working out in the bush, it was my kind of work. Art would run the chainsaw and clear what needed to be done along the road's easement. My job was to clean up the brush and branches by stacking it into piles and making it ready to run through the chipper. At day's end we'd pack up and head back to Lund. The odd time we might stop for a beer, but that was usually reserved for Friday, after our work week was complete. On those nights I'd often join Art, Milly and Henry in their favorite spot at the Lund Hotel; we always seemed to have lots to talk about.

It was now late fall, close to the end of October and that meant it was soon time for the annual Harvest Moon gathering. The Halloween dance at the town hall was always very memorable; people would dress up and come from all over. A local live band was often a significant part of the celebration; they enjoyed coming to play in Lund. The pub was full and with the town hall basically next door, people would walk back and forth between the venues until the band really got rocking. Then the bar would empty as the party moved up the hill to the hall. The dance floor was usually full and everyone would let loose and kick up their heels. There was a table set aside in the hall where people could bring food for all to snack on and the drinks served from the small makeshift bar were always reasonably priced. The hall and the pub would close at 1:00 a.m. but often people would carry on until daybreak at various houses surrounding the area. Lund was quiet the next day until around noon, as almost everyone required a little extra rest.

There were three events a year in Lund. One was in spring, another in the fall and the last gathering was the New Year's Eve celebration. While there might have been a small segment of people in Lund that you almost never saw, these socials usually brought everyone out. They were a lot of fun and in some ways helped to keep the small community closely knit. It seemed for now my life had settled into a regular routine working Monday to Friday in the bush and socializing a little on the weekends.

During the winter months it was not uncommon to see boats out in front of Lund jigging for cod or trying to troll up a winter spring for dinner. Many times, especially during the night, small schools of herring would mill about Lund harbour and Finn Bay. Percy used to go out the odd time and catch some of these fish to keep live in his bait pond. Herring was an excellent choice for catching ling cod and also could be frozen, then later on used as halibut bait. Finn Bay, where he lived, is a short distance to the north of Lund and very visible from town. It is a continuation of the mainland shore and well sheltered from almost any wind. About a dozen homes line the small cove and surround a fairly large tie-up dock in the middle of it.

Percy had a small seine net that could be set from his two-man row boat or skiff. He would locate a school with his big boat, the *Elmi*, and then he'd position the small boat where he figured the herring were going. During a flood tide the herring would sometimes move towards Finn Bay. The row boat being small and quiet improved the odds of catching something; a motor could scare the fish.

On one particular night Percy asked if I could help him catch herring by running the *Elmi*; I jumped at the opportunity.

After a brief lesson at the dock on how to run the boat I took the *Elmi* a short distance out into the bay on a trial run, then returned it to the dock and shut the motor down. Percy and another fellow had climbed into the small skiff then rowed out to the mouth of Finn Bay, waiting for the ideal moment to set their net.

The bay was dark except for a few lights reflecting from houses that lined the shore. The night air was so still you could have heard a pin drop; there was no wind and the stars were out in full display.

Percy had done this many times and knew his business. It did not take long before he spotted a school boiling near the surface, heading into the bay. He quietly slipped one end of the net into the water and, by rowing the skiff away, would form a wall in front of the fish. Continuing in this fashion he gradually encircled the net around the school. The corks that floated on the surface marked where he had started and, by joining the one end to the other, he would then "purse" the net together, thereby capturing the fish. That's what he did on this particular night but from my position I couldn't see very much at all when looking out into the blackness of the bay.

I waited, on standby, listening intently. I would be alerted to come out with the *Elmi* by either Percy's voice calling to me across the water or on a signal from his flashlight. After an hour rolled by there was still no sign for me to come; I started to wonder what was going on. Finally, much later than expected, I heard Percy call for me. I immediately fired up the *Elmi* and untied her from the moorings beside the small float, then headed out into the bay in search of the rowboat. I turned on the spot light and peered out into the night looking for the two men in the small skiff. They would be hard to see initially; the only light was the thin beam from their handheld flashlight.

I idled slowly and cautiously ahead, moving in a southerly direction searching the water. When they suddenly came into the glow of the searchlight they were a lot further away than I'd expected them to be. By now, they were halfway across Lund Harbour and seemed to be heading for Savary Island. Avoiding their net, I carefully idled up to their skiff and we tied both of the boats together. They had been in this open row boat for two hours now and it was apparent that Percy had just about enough.

The story of what happened unfolded later on. Percy had managed to encircle a sizable amount of herring in the bay with his net. It was closed up, securely wrapped around his prize, and then he started to row back to the bait pond. If he'd needed help at that point he would have let me know, but since things were going along quite smoothly, he decided not to signal. All of a sudden a large sea lion attracted by the fish surfaced and snorted right in front of the dingy; that did it. The herring in the net were scared into doing a complete reversal. Instead of going with the boat they turned and a thousand tiny tails started swimming in the opposite direction. The row boat was being towed backwards and, with the power being generated from those small fish bunched together in substantial numbers, a set of oars was not going to win the tug-of-war.

I was to learn more about the power generated from small fish in large numbers, when I heard stories about the seine boats during herring season. Unbelievable as it might sound, when there are herring openings here on the west coast, seine boats that are sixty five feet in length have actually been pulled so hard over they have been capsized by the sheer force of the small fish all going in one direction. In this case we are talking hundreds of tons of herring, in a concentrated area constituting massive amounts of power and, when spooked into diving, the result could be disastrous.

The seine boat industry began to use power skiffs to resolve the problem. These skiffs were small, open aluminum boats with huge motors. If a seine boat snagged "a large set", the power skiff attached itself to the boat amidships on the opposite side of the net and could put its powerful motor into action if needed. Pulling away from the netted fish created a balancing force and helped prevent possible mishaps. It was power against power.

On that night, however, Percy and his rowboat were dealing with a lot less power. Nonetheless, the couple of thousand small herring in his net were definitely winning the battle. Part of the problem was, of course, they had too many fish in the net. Percy eventually, after some thought, decided to briefly let one end go in order to release some of the catch, and away they swam into the depths. Now with the three of us there we started pulling the net up and then with a dip net, hand-bailed most of the fish into a live tank onboard *Elmi*. When that was almost full, and having had enough for one night, Percy decided to let go of whatever was left, then coiled the net back into the skiff.

Although it had been a partial failure this time around, a few nights later I was to witness the entire operation again and this time it worked to perfection. Percy managed to corral five hundred pounds of herring in that next set and I watched as he smoothly dragged the full net up beside the cedar lathed bait pond. Two people held each end of the seine while Percy lifted up the door to the pond. With this done, the two ends of the net were slowly opened up. The fish then trickled out of the net and swam into their new home. All this was done by using the deck lights onboard the *Elmi* and the odd handheld flashlight. When the last of the fish were in the pen, Percy closed the door and the evening's fishing was over. After everything was put away we had a beer and talked at length about the night's adventure.

The following morning Percy rolled back the netting on top of the bait pond, which was in place to keep seagulls and herons from getting at the fish. He would scoop out what he needed for the day and put them in his live tank on the *Elmi*, then head off to the cod grounds. The live tank on his boat was divided into two sections, one for the bait and the other for the lingcod. Each tank was filled with sea water; this kept both bait and catch alive, guaranteeing a fresh product delivered at trip's end.

In time, and as I got to know Percy better, I enjoyed sharing a good laugh with him. He was pretty much the only one who regularly called me "frying pan", so I needed to have something on him. I noticed sometimes when Percy delivered his catch the poundage he'd talk about later on was higher than what was actually sold, or a fish grew bigger than it really was. Observing this trend, I knew that I now had my "in". Even though most fishermen were prone to exaggerate, in Percy's case such exaggerations would soon work to my advantage. Whenever the subject of a delivery came up for discussion, and no matter who it was we'd be talking to, I would say "Is that in real pounds or Percy pounds?"

It was rare that the waters surrounding the Lund area ever got too rough. The harbour was basically very sheltered, especially from the prevailing winds that came from the northwest. A southeaster would moderately affect the area as there was little protection between Savary Island and the mainland shore. By far the worst wind was a westerly that turned more into a southwester. Although not that common it would occur when the winds blew in from the direction of Vancouver Island. Most times these westerly storms would occur in the fall and winter months. The waves would build until they hit the mainland coast and Lund would be directly affected; Hernando, Savary and Cortez Islands offered some natural protection but there was still enough distance between them and Lund to create a problem for whatever vessels were on water or tied to the dock. A floating breakwater was built in an attempt to protect the government tie-up floats in behind; they consisted of three one hundred foot fingers.

The breakwater was a big part of Lund's history. The official name for the hotel was The Lund Breakwater Inn, but most locals generally just referred to it as The Lund Hotel. Still the floating structure was a landmark. It was made from large floating steel pontoons that were heavily chained together and securely anchored to the bottom. The pontoons stretched across the harbour for about two hundred feet, allowing traffic flow inside and out at both ends. There were steel "A" frame supports that joined both sides of the pontoons together; the middle of this giant structure housed large wooden frames about six feet high above water, that extended to about eight feet below. These frames acted as a buffer against the waves, helping to weaken their power and hold back Mother Nature at her worst.

Once in a while, though, a wind would come up strong enough that made it uncomfortable being tied to the dock in Lund. In early November of that year, one such storm hit. It started early in the day and by noon had really built up. The water was white outside the breakwater with the wind gusting up to 40 knots. My boat, like the others, was at first moving gently up and down on its moorings but as the day progressed the storm worsened and the *Antique* seemed like it wanted to leap out of the water. The lines were strained severely so I doubled up the line to the bow to be extra safe. Like the others, I was hoping the wind would calm down but it soon reached the point when it was necessary to fire up the motor and get out of there. Some boats had left already and were tied up in the sheltered waters of Finn Bay. When the motor was warmed up I prepared to untie my lines, first releasing the stern line then working my way forward to release the bow. All this was not as simple as it might first appear. A big swell was running inside the harbour by now and once I rounded the corner of the breakwater, the boat would immediately be into the force of the open sea. Basically from here I would quarter bow the *Antique* into the waves and gradually ease the nose in the direction of Finn Bay, that was the plan.

I had never faced a sea as big as this in my entire first year on the *Antique*. During the fishing season, if it was too rough I was smart enough, or scared enough, not to leave the shelter of the harbour. Such days were called "Harbour Days" by fishermen. Here, however, I did not have a choice. It was time to go. Once free from the dock I put the boat in gear then proceeded broadside the length of the breakwater. The boat started to roll back and forth quite violently. Turning the corner I quickly turned the bow into the open sea. The *Antique* reared up and down; back and forth she bucked into the swell. I felt a kind of anxiety similar to my close call with the cruise ship earlier in the year. I opened the motor up to gain some ground as it seemed for a while we were standing still. Ever so slowly, the boat started to creep ahead. The sea backed down a little the closer we got to Finn Bay and eventually, half an hour later, I tied up to the float there, greatly relieved. The wind did not last into the night and I was able to return to Lund Harbour. This was a relief as there was no dock power in Finn Bay; it would have been a cold night without my heater.

Life in Lund revolved pretty much around the hotel, especially in winter. The post office and the small store both had a steady flow of people coming and going, along with the café, which always offered good home-cooked meals. With a fairly steady crowd that visited the bar, there seemed to always be someone around that you knew and could talk to. Lund was, after all, a very small but social community. It seemed hard not to know what was going on around there, and this was partly thanks to the bartenders, who I remember very well. Each one could put their own personalities on the place. There was of course Bill, who worked the day shift. I also remember his wife, Ruth, who worked at the hotel as a cook in the kitchen; they both commuted together daily. A fellow named Frank would often do the nights with Roger and Grace filling in whenever needed as well. There was usually a steady line-up of people waiting to play pool and the air was filled with the cracking sound of snooker balls. At three songs for a quarter the juke box was usually going steady. I remember John Lennon's cover of "Stand by Me" being a big favorite. There were so many other great songs then; it was the seventies after all, and everything seemed to be a hit. The pub had such a good atmosphere. In back of where the beer was served was a deep fryer; the pub's "Chicken and Jo-Jo's" platter was a fan favourite, but you could also order from the café menu.

Every now and then a large wooden vessel would tie up to the inside of the fuel dock float. It was hard to miss her arrival when she motored around the point of Sevilla Island. Her name was the Miss Clearbrook and she was clearly recognizable from a distance as she had her own distinct look. The boat was built in Powell River for prawn fishing by her owner, a fellow named

Cornie. The locals often said that the boat was built in a barn, and then they launched the barn. It's true, she was one of a kind, but the boat worked well for him and I guess that is all that really mattered. There were very few boats fishing prawns in those days and the fishery was open year round. Cornie often fished north of Lund in some of the inlets, Lochborough being one of them.

Prawns are the largest member of the west coast shrimp family and a true delicacy here on the BC coast. Cornie had a Coleman stove on his back deck where he would boil salted water in a large pot and cook the prawns he caught. After they cooled down he weighed and put them into paper bags; proudly delivering his catch in baskets to the Lund Hotel. Cornie's cooked prawns sold straight out of the pub for $2.00 per bag, which was roughly a pound.

The first time I ate them it seemed like I could not get enough. Along with a cold beer and a bit of salt they were so good. There were about 12-14 pieces per bag and, depending on how hungry I was, I could easily get through two of them at a sitting. Cornie did not stop in Lund often, maybe two or three times a year, probably on his way home. However when his boat did show up we always knew what was on the menu.

Many years later while fishing for prawns myself I remember seeing the name Miss Clearbrook 67 painted in white paint on a rock bluff near Lasqueti Island. Though the name had faded over the years it was still recognizable and seeing it would always take me back to my days in Lund and those delicious bags of prawns. I asked someone one day about the boat and was told that she had sank, a while ago now, somewhere off the waters in front of Lund. Everyone got safely off, but still it was a sad ending to the Miss Clearbrook.

Sometime during the middle of December that year we got our first snowfall. The timing could not have been better because Art and I had just finished the job at Okeover and it would have been dangerous to work in the bush with snow on the ground. Usually it didn't last too long at sea level but a cold spell had descended on the coast that stayed with us for a while.

Next day an entire foot of snow fell, changing the scenery in the small town and the surrounding area. It was beautiful. Everyone had a boost of energy from the white stuff. Snowball fights and long walks in the area became everyday occurrences. The boats and the dock area made for a postcard scene. I did not mind the snow, being accustomed to it growing up in Southern Ontario. Like it or not, for me, it was a nice change from the rain.

The walk from the dock to Chris and Dianna's place was about two miles. The small house they rented was tucked in behind Finn Bay on a seldom travelled area close to town, called Baggi Road. This was where I spent Christmas that year. Those like myself, whose families were far away, grouped together and had a quiet, holiday celebration. The snow seemed to remind me of home, as we often had a white Christmas in Hamilton. Even though it was not the first time away from my family during Christmas, I still felt a little homesick; so many good memories came back to me then. That afternoon I phoned home and talked to them; it helped to pick up my spirits.

All in all we had a great Christmas in Lund the year of 1975 and three days later, on the 28th, I celebrated my 24th birthday. We anxiously awaited the arrival of the New Year and for me, as always, it brought hope and optimism. Lund had a big New Year's Eve party at the hall and the next day the hotel set up a huge brunch in the dining room. Later on there was an all-you-could-eat buffet as well. A great way to end the day and start off the new year; the food, especially the roast beef dinner, was so good.

There seems to be something special about the start of a new year and 1976 was no exception. It was still only early January, yet already I had a hard time sleeping some nights in anticipation of the upcoming salmon season. I set about organizing a schedule around the list of items and repairs that my boat needed. I definitely needed a better way to communicate when on the water. What I'd had to work with for my first year was basically nothing. On a trip to Powell River I picked up a small CB radio from the local electronics shop. They were relatively inexpensive then and had up to 40 channels but were good for only short distances. Still, all in all, it beat the heck out of a megaphone.

With Art's help, I decided it was now time to select a new set of trolling poles. He knew where there was a nice stand of small, straight firs not very far from where we had worked that fall. We arrived at the spot in his truck and within a short time I had picked out two nice trees. Art cut them both down with his chain saw and then bucked each one off at a length of twenty-five feet. He lent me his draw knife for peeling the bark off and in a short while they were skinned, looking new and shiny. We then loaded them into Art's truck and took them to his place for drying. The rule of thumb was that trolling poles were usually fitted to the length of the boat they were going on. The *Antique* was twenty-eight feet long so they were cut at twenty-five feet. A forty foot boat, then, would have longer poles, gauged close to a one to one ratio.

As usual money could be a little thin before the season started. Like most fishermen, I again would require a line of credit in order to purchase fishing supplies. With Chris needing to "gear up" also, we decided to take a trip to the big city of Vancouver, where I reopened my line of credit at John Redden Net Company. After Chris filled out his application form, we were allowed to charge any gear needed, up to a certain limit of course. Nothing had changed much from the previous year. There was still row after row of everything you could need for all types of fishing, be it trolling, gillnetting or seining. If anything, the aisles seemed even longer than I remembered. There was a list of items I really could use, so I started at the top by first picking up new trolling wire and cannon balls. I spent a lot of time looking over the hoochies and spoons, selecting out the ones I remembered worked best for me the previous year. Chris would say, "Try this one, it worked well for so-and-so last year." I decided to try one or two new items but not too many, as I had found out in my first year, what works well for one person may not work well for you. Funny how it could be that way.

What I did do, however, was to stop buying just one or two of an item, instead I would buy a whole box. Flashers and spoons came in one dozen boxes, while plugs were usually six to a box. There was the usual large selection of spoons, more than you would find in most places, but I narrowed it down to what had previously caught fish for me. They came in all different sizes and colours. Spoons could be straight chrome or half and half splits of chrome/brass, copper/brass, copper, brass and so on. I had found the Wonder spoons worked well for me and so I bought several boxes of size 5.5 and 6, brass and brass chrome. Of course you need the proper hook size and type to fit the size of each spoon. This is critical to the action created by the lure when it moves through the water. I would use a fairly heavy hook for the Wonder spoon; usually a number eight triple X blue and I bought two boxes of those. I needed perlon, snaps, stop rings and ganion twine. I could have gone on forever. Being not a big fan of shopping in general, I must say that going through that store was a lot of fun.

However, like the previous year, reality hits you when the orders are tallied up. After I had signed on the dotted line, I walked out $800 dollars later with the equivalent of one cardboard box and two small bags. Chris and I then sat in the car going over everything to be sure it was all there. It was a lot of money to me then, the total being roughly a quarter of what I had grossed in my first year of fishing, but I needed the gear. No gear basically meant no fish, and that was the bottom line. Chris spent nearly the same amount that day as he needed a fair bit to get going his first year. In good faith, the store manager tossed in a couple of white high liner fishing caps for free, the kind that John and many others often wore. As the story goes, the hats were handed out years ago to the boat and the crew that had landed the biggest halibut seasons, in recognition of their accomplishments. For now, the high production part did not apply to me but nonetheless, I sized the strap at the back of the cap and slid it on my head. *Maybe one day I will be the 'high' boat,* I thought to myself. I wore that type of cap for many years; it suited me and became a part of my every day attire. I made sure there was always one for when I was fishing and a clean one for when I was not. John would refer to that as your 'town hat'.

We arrived back in Lund late that evening, the round trip to Vancouver being an all-day affair. I stored my gear aboard the boat and went to bed. Tomorrow was a new day and with it already planned out, I would need an early start.

After breakfast next morning I set about putting my new steel trolling wire onto the gurdies: off with the old and on with the new. This job takes a little time but soon enough all four gurdies were complete. Next I attached the cannon balls onto the spliced wire ends, joining the two together with fresh green ganion twine. I wrapped all the loose ends of twine neatly with black electrician's tape; everything had to be just so. I wanted this new season to start off, in all aspects, on the right track. Any small things I'd learned from my first year came naturally to me this second time around, but I still double checked everything to be sure anyways.

It was now time to tackle the big job of installing the new trolling poles. They'd been drying for a month by now; with help, I moved them down to the float and laid them beside the *Antique.* I took down the old ones and stripped them of all the gear. Then I re-attached all the collars in the same place on the new ones, so they would work the same as the old. I fastened new springs on the ends, getting rid of the old, stretched, and rusted ones. Next I attached the pulley and blocks to the collars; these are important when raising and lowering the poles. I had cut a notch at the base of the pole so it would rest on the half inch bolt and pole bracket that supported it; this basically works in a pendulum motion. Once one side was ready to go, I laid the pole perpendicular to my boat and with help from Art and Henry I lifted the one end and placed the notch over the bolt. I ran the new pull-up lines through the blocks on the mast and guided them to the deck of the boat and made ready to raise the pole into the cross tree. One person lifted the pole in the middle while I yarded on the ropes. It slid with ease into its proper place. I tied off the pull-up lines to a cleat on the mast, securing it in place. The galvanized cable stay lines front and back dangled like spaghetti but by pulling down I was able to join each of them to the boat, with heavy chain and shackles on either end. They were slack but in place and by adjusting the turn buckles I was able to firm up the rigging. After that I attached the tag lines that were fastened to the springs and, taking the other ends, I connected them with light ganion to a stop-ring on the trolling wire.

I had left the poles as bare wood with no paint. This was unlike the old ones and it definitely gave the boat a fresh look. By early the next day I had the second pole up and in place; this went easier than the first, as I now knew what needed to be done. With the second set of tag lines hooked up, I felt a feeling of accomplishment. It was another step towards being ready.

Chris was busy doing a little mechanical work on his boat. The *Neptune* had a gas motor with a wet exhaust system; it was quite different than my little diesel motor. Chris being mechanically inclined, installed new plugs then adjusted the timing so the engine ran like a clock. At this time of year there were a few other local boats in Lund getting ready, including the *Lucky Lady Four* and *Shrub Isle*. Bill and George were busy at their shipyard with other vessels needing work done. There always seemed to be someone on dry dock; it could be a new plank was needed or maybe just general maintenance required. Boats do need a lot of attention, but the train of thought is, if you look after them, they "look after you".

My haul out was booked and hopefully all I would need was a fresh coat of copper paint and new zincs. These products I purchased at Lund Marine. Jens always had a good supply in stock and his store was handy, being located right there in the small harbour. They also had a marine ways, but this dry dock was bigger than the one at Sevilla Island and capable of hauling out many of the larger vessels in the area, including tugs.

All in all, the little town of Lund seemed especially busy at this time of year. There was always something on the go, be it fishing, logging, beach combing or construction projects on nearby islands. At night everyone would gather at the bar and talk about their day, often sharing what still needed to be done and discussing what had been accomplished. It was a great time to be part of this small community. Things were bustling and everyone seemed happy.

My next task was to build a small box that would fit into the hold on the *Antique* in order to pack ice and fish. The hold was virtually non-existent, being very shallow and small. Most of that area had bits and pieces of used equipment, old rope and some portions of chain. The addition of this item was an important one as it would enable me to stay overnight in an anchorage. Also, it cut back on the daily travelling time, so I'd save some fuel as well as gain fishing time. I would not need it in the Gulf of Georgia most likely, as there were plenty of fish buying stations at hand; but it would certainly help when I moved north to Port Hardy.

A few days later I finished a plywood box that was large but practical enough for my purposes. It fit nicely into the existing fish hold and stood about two feet above deck level. Though not huge in size because of limited space, I still estimated it could hold about twenty fish; that would not be a bad delivery at all. I fitted a drain plug on one side at the base, to release any melted ice water that would accumulate. I would use ice blankets for some of the inside insulation and a couple of small pieces of foam covered in plywood acted as insulation for the top of the box. When it was finished I painted the inside with white primer and then, with weather cooperating, I added two coats of non-toxic fish hold enamel. The box shone a bright white when it was finished and would easily pass any inspection. With that job completed I went to work sanding down my checkers and adding a fresh coat of white enamel there as well. Any places on the boat that came into contact with fish were now completed.

In early March I received by mail my application form for the boat's annual insurance policy. It arrived addressed to my name c/o my official mail box: General Delivery, Lund. As in the previous year, the vessel value had basically stayed the same. A percentage of that value was multiplied by a set rate number and that total was the boat's insurance premium fee for the year. The government's "Fishing Vessel Insurance Plan" again worked well for me and many others. It was the most affordable way to go in protecting your investment. All this had to be in place by the end of March when the previous year's plan expired.

The insurance inspector arrived about a week later; it was the same person as the year before so we were familiar with each other. I was fourth in line and shook his hand as he boarded the *Antique*. All seemed to be ready for him, and I definitely felt more confident about the procedure this time around. He asked a few questions while making sure the bilge pumps were working properly, then checked to see that all other safety items were in place and in good order. After about fifteen minutes of going through the boat inside and out he signed off on the necessary papers, I had passed once again.

In Lund we worked together as much as possible, especially when it came to certain aspects of the industry. So when enough fishermen had their vessels ready for fish hold inspection, we contacted the local fisheries officer in Powell River and set a date for him to come and check our boats. As the weather had remained above seasonal for this time year, most of us were ready for him and a couple of days later he arrived in Lund. Much like the insurance agent he made his way in an orderly fashion from boat to boat. He'd take a close look at fish holds and checkers, being sure all was clean and in good order; the *Antique* was washed and ready. I passed the inspection easily, another necessary item now out of the way. A few days later my B Licence renewal form arrived by mail from Vancouver. With this important document filled out, and after I had paid the $10.00 to renew, I was officially legal to catch salmon for the 1976 season.

It was now early in April and the tides were favourable for the one big job that still needed to be done, the annual haul out. I was ready to go when my time finally arrived. After securing the boat in place, Bill fired up the winch. I gave him the thumbs-up, then he engaged the clutch and slowly the boat, riding on rail tracks, was pulled by a steel cable toward shore and onto dry land. I set right to work because I did not have that much time to get everything finished. After I'd scrubbed hard to remove the barnacles and bottom growth from the hull, Bill had a quick look then decided to add a bit of caulking along both garboard seams. They are the planks closest to the keel. All the other seams looked good and after he'd caulked that area he added cement to seal it. He would mix a little bit of baking soda to the cement, helping it to harden up faster. Once this was done I painted the bottom with copper paint, checked and cleaned the cooling pipes with rough sand paper and replaced both zincs. There was also a round zinc that was fastened around the shaft close to the propeller and it gave further protection to that area; this I replaced as well. It was a full day's work, but a very important one; I was glad to have it over with. There were still the top sides of the boat to be sanded and painted, but that would have to wait for now. The weather needed to warm up a bit first to make working on that part of the boat a little more ideal.

Although my to-do list was complete, work on the *Antique* never seemed to end. When you thought that all was ready and ahead of schedule, something else would pop up. I was still tinkering with some things right up until opening day, setting and lubricating the brakes on the gurdies being one of them. I also set about tying extra gear, especially flashers and hoochies, to have ready for the inevitable snarls and tangles. This would save a lot of time, especially if the bite was on.

The goal at this time of year was to have a day or two off before the long season started but over the thirty years that I trolled for salmon, I don't recall ever having the luxury of a pre-season day off, no matter how soon I began. We did, however, manage to squeeze in a celebration night a couple of days before the start. Many of us got together and let loose a little. It was something I believe we all needed, and helped to ease some tensions. This gathering was kind of a tradition and it happened in most ports up and down the coast prior to opening day.

With that out of my system I rested for quite a while the next day but still managed to find a few small things to do. I was in bed early only to toss and turn for most of the night; another restless sleep, but at least the long wait was finally over.

Lots of Fish

Opening day, April 15th, 1976. There was no need for the alarm to sound; I was out of bed at 4 am. I flicked on my cabin light and made a few things ready below, in preparation to leave. It was still dark and the air outside was crisp. With no wind, conditions were ideal to start the season. A few lights were on in other boats as they prepared their morning coffee. I had a glass of orange juice and climbed out on deck. After a long stretch and yawn I washed my face and hands, brushed my teeth and slipped back inside.

I went through the morning ritual of checking oil levels in

both motor and gear even though I'd already done that the night before, then started the motor. After a few minutes of warming up, I untied the boat and slowly idled out and around the breakwater.

I quickly lowered the polls into place then watched the Ekolite sounder flash away, its red blips clearly seen in the dark hours of morning. As the bottom started to fall away I made ready to go to the stern. A year's experience really helped as I pretty much knew the problem areas, especially the shallower spots. It was 4:20 and the first faint glow of morning light was starting to appear; I was the first boat on the tack. I engaged the clutch that drove the gurdies and then, moving to the stern, started to lower the first cannonball into the water.

Down into the depths went the first piece of gear, that being a plug just above the lead, and then, missing one set of marks, I snapped on the second piece of gear, a Hot Spot flasher with a hoochie behind it. The new wire was marked at 2½ fathoms and I continued the same pattern, snapping on a third and final piece to complete the line. I continued to lower the lead to a depth of 20 fathoms and then I snapped on the float that moved the line a safe distance behind where it would not tangle with my forward or deep line. When in position and far enough back, I attached the stop ring that would take the tag line out to its furthest place on the pole. With this done, the float was now where it needed to be. Then I disengaged that gurdie, put the break on, and made ready to drop the deep line in on that same side of the boat. I had a quick look around, checking the

flasher with a hoochie

sounder, and after taking my bearings saw that everything seemed fine so I continued about my business. The other three lines went out smoothly and soon all were in place. I had put three pieces of gear on the pig lines and four on each deep line. After that I went into the wheel house and adjusted the throttle further so the fishing gear would have the proper action to entice the fish into biting. Speed was so critical and something you had to constantly keep an eye on. I attached a flasher to one of the deep lines right below the surface so it was visible from the wheelhouse and deck area. The speed at which it turned told me all was fine below and made for a better opportunity to catch fish.

I headed to the first point on Sevilla Island, which marked the beginning of the Ragged Island tack. The sounder flashed red as it picked up a school of herring just below the surface then, looking up, I saw two lines start to pull hard on the springs, both on the same side. Alright, fish on. I brought the deep line up and on the first piece of gear pulled in a lively ten pound spring salmon to the stern of the boat. Then reaching down I gently removed the hook and released him back into the water. The rule of thumb was, it is good luck to release your first fish of the year, and this I did. There was nothing on the rest of that line so I lowered it back down and once back in place, started to bring in the back line. I coiled the first two pieces of gear into the boat and continued to raise the lead until the snap just broke the surface of the water. The line was pulling hard under the strain of a fighting fish and when I grabbed the perlon it was tight, straight out and hard away from the boat. It was a good sized fish and slowly I guided it towards me. It took a few more short runs and then lay on its side, tired from the struggle.

I reached for my gaff and a moment later I had landed my first fish of the year. A beautiful seventeen pound spring salmon lay in the checkers of my boat; what a good start.

I had room to make a turn and headed back up the beach to repeat the process over again. In almost the same spot I had two more lines go. I straightened out the boat a little and, being sure of where I was, pointed the bow back into the beach in an attempt to grab a few more. Looking out from the back of my wheelhouse I saw the starboard pig float bobbing up and down in the water signaling that another fish had taken a hook. *This is what it's all about,* I thought and about halfway down the tack I quickly moved to the stern to start bringing the first line in. There were two fish on that line; a double header. Overall and on that pass I took five more fish off the gear. They were mixed sizes but that did not matter to me: as long as they were over twenty-six inches in length they were legal.

As the sun started to show itself on the horizon, I stared with pride at the morning's catch so far. Ten shiny, bright spring salmon lay in the checkers; this certainly was a better start than the previous year. I tacked back down and outside of the boats that had the right of way.

I now had time to start cleaning some of the fish I'd caught and wondered to myself what colour their flesh would be. Colour meant a big difference in price per pound. The public traditionally wanted the predominant orange-red flesh colour common to all Pacific salmon. The colour does not really affect the actual taste of the fish but is basically a marketing ploy. Many fishermen would tell you that the less common white spring salmon are slightly oilier than those with deeper colour and made for a better smoked product. However that did not reflect in the actual price. Regardless, when cleaning spring salmon it always made me a little happier when they were orange or red. I have seen salmon that were actually marbled, having a mixture of both orange and white. This would often lead to arguments between the fisherman and the buyer as to what the grade of the salmon should be. Once all my fish were dressed, I saw that I had only one white spring for the morning so far, and that put an even brighter shine to my day. I scanned the water to assess the tack and counted about a dozen boats between the Ragged Islands and the Iron Mines. Most were local, but there were a couple of boats from out of town. There was plenty of room and we were not overcrowded. I waved to the other boats I passed that were trolling in the other direction. Many of the skippers gave me the thumbs up sign. Most of them were in their sterns and that usually indicated activity of some kind, either cleaning or pulling fish aboard.

Again I trolled through a large ball of small herring that had boiled up to the surface and had a crystal clear view of it all as the water still remained flat calm. I caught four more fish that morning and then from 10:00 am to 12:00 noon never had another bite. I picked up my gear shortly after and headed towards Lund to deliver my morning's catch. There was one boat ahead of me already and when it pulled away I moved up beside the small Nor-Pac fish scow.

It was the same buyer from the previous year and Chuck quickly grabbed one of my lines and helped tie me up. We exchanged greetings and I proudly started to pass the cleaned and washed fish from my checkers to the shiny white cement floor of the barge. He had what they called a fish pew in his hands, basically a long wooden handle with a sharp steel point on one end. Chuck would put it through the head of the fish then lift it into stainless steel tubs that hung from the weighing scales; he could tell sizes by just generally looking at the fish. Spring salmon that were five to seven pounds were small; eight-twelve were medium, twelve pounds and over were large. Of course he also had to look at the colour, then each fish was tallied on a piece of paper before being totalled and written down on your sales slip.

I was given a fish book from the company that recorded the weights and prices of each delivery. We could take cash or "book" your fish, or a combination of both. If you booked you were paid later and you would receive price adjustments that might come between delivery and payment day. At times you would have a fish that might weigh eleven and a half pounds and it was up to Chuck as to whether you would get the large size grade. Sometimes you did and sometimes you didn't. But it usually all worked out in the end. The price per pound was always the main topic of conversation on opening day. This year they were not too bad at all: large red was $2.50 a pound, medium $1.85 a pound and small $1.50 a pound. All white spring salmon, regardless of size were $1.00 a pound, so you can see what a big difference the colour of the flesh could make. I had four large, seven mediums, and three small salmon for the morning bite and there was only one white salmon among them. My catch totalled a little over $200 dollars and I was happy. It was my first real taste of money coming in—instead of going out—in a while. Once unloaded, I pulled away from the fish buying station and tied back up to the government float. I shut the motor down, sat in my small chair, and started going over my fish slip, reflecting on the day so far. Several other boats were already tied up ahead of me and many were exchanging their thoughts on the morning's adventures; the dock was full of talk. Catches were compared and stories told, always a great pastime that most of us enjoyed.

I was curious about how Chris had made out and when he tied up I walked over to have a chat. Diana had gone out fishing with him and they were both happy as the boat had run well and they'd caught some fish, a great combination at any time. The three of us walked to the café to have lunch. I was starving and ordered my usual, the Lund burger with fries; you could never go wrong with that meal. Basically, lunch was my first full meal of the day. Orange juice, an apple, or a banana had to carry me till then. My motor ran pretty much on adrenalin then, cooking on my Coleman stove was not an option. There were always more important things that had to be done besides eating. After lunch I returned to my boat to change some gear and get ready for the night bite. I selected a few more of the hoochies that had worked well during the morning. The lures that had caught fish would replace the gear that had not. However, the constant challenge was, what worked one time, may not necessarily produce the next. It was always a bit of a 'chess match' to determine what colour or type of gear the fish might prefer each day.

Everyone had their own theories on this of course, and the topic always made for a great debate. I had learned that whatever blended in best with the water seemed to catch fish. So in clear water I went with more green and blues and for water that was cloudier I used browns and yellows with a white belly on the hoochie. I liked my set up and had confidence that it worked for me, that being three to four pieces of gear on each deep line and two to three pieces on each back line. Once I found out where the fish were biting I would raise and lower everything accordingly. Early morning was usually shallower and as the day progressed the fish moved deeper. All seemed ready for the afternoon/night bite. I would have an hour's rest prior to heading back out.

At 4:00 o'clock I started up the engine and idled out of the breakwater; debating on whether I should go right or left from there. Right was the Ragged Island's tack and left was the Iron Mines. I decided to try the Iron Mines this time and so I set my gear at thirty fathoms. As I approached the tack I sat in the wheel house with my eyes fixed on the sounder. I was not as familiar with this place and it was not my favorite spot; however, I reasoned that it was probably best to learn as many tacks as possible. The cliff face here fell sharply down to the water where it continued to the sea floor; you could almost rub the tips of the poles along the rock bluffs, the edge was that steep. There was the odd boulder you would have to swing out on but basically it was fairly easy fishing with few hang-ups. The first pass yielded nothing, but on the way back I picked up a nice ten pounder. I noticed that I was alone here, as most of the other boats had gone back to the Ragged Islands. I really did not like fishing in too big of a crowd and it was nice to have this much room here. I tried two more passes and only picked up one small fish. With that I decided to make a long one way tack in the direction of the Raggeds and join the others. It would take roughly thirty minutes to get there, depending of course on the tide.

Upon arriving, I angled the *Antique* towards the first point and immediately both deep lines started to bang away. This was more like it! I passed a few other boats going in the opposite direction and everyone seemed to be busy. Chris was there and I saw him land a nice fish outside of me. He pointed to where I was, indicating that this was the hot spot. It was hard to read the bottom here as there was a massive ball of feed directly under the boat. But knowing I was close to a shallow spot, I angled out in anticipation of it and sped up a little, in order to raise the gear over the reef. As the edge fell off I idled back to normal trolling speed and went to the stern in hopes that the fish were still on. Sometimes, when you speed up like that, you could tear the hook from the fish's mouth, especially if it is barely hooked. This did not happen here and I landed two beauties, one off each side, a twelve and fourteen pounder. My first thought was *How much had I missed here?* As I trolled by Chris again he held up two hands signalling ten fish. Boy, did I make the wrong turn for the evening bite. Oh well, that can happen. I made a few more quick passes in at the point, being careful not to cut in front of anybody or push them off their tack. These maneuvers produced five more springs for my effort, making a total of nine fish altogether. As the sun started to set on that day I made my final tack toward the Lund Harbour to sell. I discovered that Chris had a nice round dozen, as did several other boats, which proved how critical "being in the right spot at the right time" can be. Of course the luck factor had something to do with it, too, and everyone usually had their day. Once tied up and things were shut down, a few of us went up to the pub to talk about the day's fishing. Everyone had their own story and after a couple of beers those tales, as usual, seemed to get even better. So and so had a big day and you would feel like you had missed out. My day's total seemed to be above average, not quite enough to put me into "top boat" category; I was content.

We all had our competitive edge and I think this was part of the process that made us become more successful fishermen. After all, everyone wanted to be the high liner of the day, me included. Not doing so well one day certainly inspired you to try harder the next, but someone would always seem to catch "one more" than you, regardless of the truth. Such rivalry made for good jostling and it seemed Chris and I always had our own little personal competition going on, "if he caught four then I caught five" kind of thing and on it would go, back and forth. It worked both ways, this kind of teasing, and was fine as long as you were fairly close in overall numbers. There were times, though, when you would get beaten badly and those days were not a whole lot of fun, so we had to know when to rake it in. All of us had our turn at being top boat and I must say whenever it happened for me, it was very satisfying.

Lyman

It was about the fourth or fifth day into the start of the season when I met a fellow by the name of Lyman in the Lund café. He enthusiastically said hello; I guessed him to be about five years older than me. He'd probably overheard some of us talking about the morning's bite and decided he really wanted to see this for himself. Lyman was sitting with a lady who, I later learned, was his brother's wife. After a brief introduction, I offered to take him out fishing with me that afternoon. When finished with lunch, I showed them where the *Antique* was tied up and on parting company, I told him to be there by 4:00pm. Lyman lived a short distance from downtown Lund on a small farm with his family, probably about a twenty minute walk from the docks.

He arrived 15 minutes early and I helped him aboard the boat. There was not a lot of room for two people on the *Antique* at one time. After a brief rundown of everything on board I decided the safest and best place for him was to sit on the new hatch cover, where he had a bird's eye view of everything. I started up the motor and we idled out of the harbour. I engaged the drive to my gurdies and told Lyman not to get too close to any of the moving parts that were on deck. The drive shaft on the port side that ran to the gurdies transmission was my biggest concern.

"OK, David," he said, and this more formal approach was how he would always refer to me. For Lyman, it was always the full form, but being used to "Dave", "Antique Dave", or "Frying Pan Dave" for so long, I was surprised by the expression. But I liked it. Lyman's brother was of the same name, and I figured that was how he addressed him as well.

It was a pleasant change having company on board and as I went about my business in the stern, Lyman carefully and intensely watched everything I did. I explained some of the things to him as I was putting my gear into the water. He listened closely and asked only the odd question. It was certainly a different world out here on the ocean and by now I was already taking it a little for granted. But it was a brand new experience for Lyman and he could hardly contain his excitement when I landed a fish. He would stand up to get a better view when I was fighting a fish in the stern and when it came aboard the boat he would yell out, "That's a beauty, it's bigger than the last one." I fished until 8:30pm and caught five spring salmon total; not too bad at all. We returned to harbour, sold the fish and then I tied the boat up to the float. Work was not over yet, as I scrubbed out the checkers so they would be shiny clean for tomorrow. Lyman stayed, quietly watching, wanting to help wherever; I could tell he really liked fishing.

Lyman's brother and sister-in-law came over to see us after we'd tied up. I introduced myself and gave them a quick tour of everything. I am sure they wanted to be confident that Lyman was safe when onboard the boat and I assured them that he had been. I pointed out the extra life jacket and told them I would keep an extra careful eye on him when on the boat. As Lyman started to head back home with his family, he paused and asked, "Could I come out for the morning bite, David?" I said, "Sure, you just have to be here by 4:30a.m."

Still in bed next morning, I felt the boat list as someone stepped onboard. It was Lyman. "Good Morning David," he said from the cabin doorway.

"I'll be right there, Lyman," I replied as I crawled out from beneath the warm blankets. It was 4:00a.m. I moved out on deck and said, "Give me a minute to wake up and go through my morning procedure; I'll be right with you."

He stepped back onto the dock and gave me a little space to go about my business. I noticed he had packed a lunch kit. He was ready to go. Myself, I did not really function well until I had thoroughly washed my face with cold water and brushed my teeth, then I was ready to start the day. Lyman watched closely from the door as I checked the engine and all the other mechanical components. Then I fired the motor up. Lyman took his seat on the hatch cover while I untied the boat and within five minutes, after idling out past the breakwater, I took my place in the stern. Daylight was just breaking and the early morning seemed to give a whole new perspective to everything. Neither of us said a word as I set my gear, then watched my sounder and the ends of my poles for any sign of action. I explained to Lyman how this part of fishing worked and right at that moment, the deep line started to move. The spring moved in and out, indicating that a pretty good size fish had taken the hook and was fighting to get free. Lyman now knew what to look for. Watching the springs and the lines after that became his job and I do not think he ever missed a one. The first fish was a nice 15 pounder; a great way to start the day.

As we carried on fishing through to the end of the Ragged Island's tack I picked up two more salmon along the way. "There's one on that deep line," Lyman said and, sure enough, there was. His keen watch proved especially helpful when my attention was turned to cleaning fish or attending to other things in the stern. We had a good morning and there was not one fish that came aboard without a huge grin from Lyman. His vivid descriptions led me to believe every fish for him was an adventure and he helped to bring a smile to my face. He loved this as much as I did. When the bite slowed down a little, around 10:00 o'clock, Lyman opened up his lunch kit and had something to eat, closely watching all the while as I went about my business.

So it happened that Lyman fished with me off and on over

the next couple of weeks. He would come out for two days in a row then maybe miss a day, but usually he let me know in advance when he could be there. Regardless, it was always great when he showed up and joined me for the day's fishing. In some ways I guess you could say Lyman was my first deck hand but I always referred to him then as a fishing partner. His positive enthusiasm certainly carried through to me at the time; even on a slow day he was a treat to have aboard. Those magical fishing times that we shared together, so many years ago now, have never been forgotten.

The word had filtered back to us in Lund that fishing was apparently good all through the Gulf of Georgia that spring of 1976. Many boats had not travelled through from Vancouver or ports south of us yet, preferring to stay closer to their home harbours.

A little over a week into the season, however, a few more vessels slowly began to appear on the scene. *Stormin Norman* had bought the *Essie T* from Paul who in turn had purchased another boat. A local fellow named Brian acquired the *Sea Maid* from Dan, who now owned a thirty-nine foot vessel called the *Miss Kelly*. Most of these boats were step-ups for the skippers and each owner seemed proud of their new acquisitions.

Some familiar faces started to arrive in small groups over the next few weeks, many in the same vessels they'd had the previous year. There was the *Ern*, *Adella P*, and the *Cathy Bell* that I recognized from the year before. Some of the other people and boats I recall from that season are Ron and Kit on the *Debbie*, Jerry on the *Pescawa*, Frank on the *Sola*, George Kelly and Mark on the *Auriga*, my old friend Rob Kelly on the *Betty M 11* and his brother Chris, who still owned *The Comet*. Most of these people stopped over in Lund; it did seem like the last stepping stone on their way to the north coast. A few fished for a little while, others only stayed the night; certainly not an uncommon thing at this time of the year.

I remember one day, while trolling directly in front of Lund, a beautiful forty-two foot troller glided by inside of me on its way to the north coast. The name on the bow read *Fan Isle* and was owned by a fellow named Bill, from Powell River. To me, it had the best lines I had ever seen on a vessel and I thought of owning a boat like that one day myself. You could fish anywhere on the coast and comfortably take the weather with something of her size. I knew it would take some time; for now, it was only a distant dream as I watched her slowly motor out of sight.

One of the boats returning to Lund from the year before was the *Marla*. The thirty-two foot troller was built and owned by a fellow named Berger. He would leave his home port of Vancouver and slowly work his way up the gulf, eventually winding up in Lund. Berger was a very quiet man, probably in his seventies then. He was very sharp and spoke with a slight Norwegian accent. Every morning he was up early like the rest of us getting ready to start his day on the water. He loved fishing. In time, it also became apparent that he had something special going on. Berger may not have caught the *most* fish on any given day but more often than not he would deliver the *largest*. We could only guess at how he did it. Did he have the right gear? Was it the boat or a secret spot? None of us could figure it out.

The *Marla* was a very shallow drafted craft and hence a little tender in the water, but very quiet. When Berger started his engine you hardly knew it was running.

A rock at about the mid-way point of the Ragged Islands tack marked the place where most of us would turn around and start back the other way, or we might carry on a little further up the gut, where it narrowed, before turning. Inside that rock it was tight and could shallow up quickly; Berger was usually the only one to attempt going in there. You had to manoeuver in a very small area here; though others would try, it rarely produced anything for them. However, if there was a twenty-pound-plus spring salmon lurking nearby, Berger, it seemed, would most often get it. Some fishermen would say they knew when Berger had a big one on, as the *Marla* would rock back and forth ever so slightly. It was definitely an art form and a challenge, this cat and mouse game, which evolved from scratching the rocks for spring salmon and was something that he really relished.

Around this time the fifty-two foot troller, *Prince of Denmark* arrived in Lund. Peter and Dave had just left the Vancouver shipyard where they had spent the winter making a few additions to her there before starting their second season with the boat. They stopped for a couple days in Lund, being their home port, and I had a chance to look her over up close. *What a contrast to the* Antique, I thought; she had a new onboard freezer system along with a huge fish hold. You could stay out as long as you wanted in that boat, making it ideal for salmon and the growing off-shore tuna fishery. In later years, when bigger money entered into the coastal fisheries, there would be many more vessels of her size built, but at the time, the *Prince of Denmark* was one of the first.

There was the odd day when production seemed to drop off in Lund, but overall fishing held up well that year. It was certainly not hard to do better than the season before, that's for sure.

Tides and weather can affect fishing dramatically and by the end of April we were nearing a full moon, which meant bigger tides. The feed, and consequently salmon, can be pushed around more by the stronger currents when this happens. Fishing had dropped off dramatically and I wondered if this was the end of it. Then, on top of it all, the winds blew from the southeast for two full days, raining heavily off and on. Catching four or five fish each day during this foul weather did nothing to improve my mood. It had been several weeks of a steady grind so after a one-fish morning bite I decided to take the afternoon off. A few other fishermen with the same idea tied up as well, then we headed up to the Lund Pub together. It was a rare break and one, I think, that was needed. It's amazing what a warm, dry atmosphere can do for your morale, along with good food, games of pool and music. We enjoyed the moment and our spirits were lifted. At around dusk the wind stopped and clearer skies to the west signalled an impending weather change. Shortly thereafter I headed back down to my boat and packed it in for the night. I remember hearing the wind blowing hard from the northwest most of that evening as I slowly drifted off to sleep.

I awoke to a very still morning; no rain or wind, and the water was glassy smooth. Heading out early, I lowered my gear into the still depths and slowly took a course for the Ragged Islands. Having barely finished my morning's orange juice I looked out and saw the springs on both deep lines moving back and forth, signaling I had fish. This looked promising. I pulled five fish in on my first tack up and down. *Maybe the fish were here but have been off the bite?"* I thought. Regardless, whatever it was worked in my favour; it would be my best day yet. All told, between the morning and evening bites, I caught forty-five spring salmon worth a total of $850. I think I was in a bit of shock, having made so much money in just one day. To top it off I was also high boat, and I'm sure I wore my white cap a little more proudly on my head; it was my turn.

Spring (Chinook) salmon

The next day yielded almost the same result with a total of forty-two spring salmon caught, worth $800: two big back-to-back days. I took some cash and booked the rest of my deliveries, meaning the company would send me a cheque later on with the balance owed. I had a huge roll of money in my pants pocket when I walked up to the bar after that second day of fishing. In the Lund Pub there was a bell you could sound when someone decided to buy a round for the house. I rang it. It was the one and only time I ever did. The place was buzzing, as everyone had enjoyed a pretty good couple of days on the water, and it was standing room only. Bad time to be buying for the house, I guess, but it didn't matter, it was something I wanted to do.

Up until now it was one of the high points of my young career and it gave me a catch number to strive for. Fishing had always been fun but I believe my thought process changed a little after that; for the first time I realized that there was money to be made here as well. Making money doing something you loved. Now that's a bonus.

Although fishing slowed down a little after that, I noticed a change in myself. I seemed far more confident than before and good things, as I'd been told, can come from that attitude. It felt to me like I was starting to get it. The type and colour of gear, the ever-so-critical right boat speed for trolling and so many other things I had been learning, now seemed to come naturally. I was flying through the gear. Up a line would come, the fish cleaned off, and quickly back down it went. This maximized my overall catching capability, especially when the bite was on. Those two days in May, 1976 were a turning point for me and after that, I never looked back.

It did not take long for word to get out and a few more boats started to appear on the tack. One day we had up to twenty-five of us fishing in the area. Production dropped accordingly and many boats drifted on, heading north around the middle of May. There was still enough fish right here, however, to keep me interested and I decided to stay in the general area into early June, still lots of time yet before making the big jump to the north country. I wanted to be sure that everything on the *Antique* was in good working order before it was time for me to leave.

Regardless, Chris and I decided to set a departure date fairly soon that would work the best for us. I had the benefit of having made the trip the previous year and although I'd done it only once, it still made for a wealth of knowledge. All the anxieties and fears I had from my first year would not be as significant this second time around; there was now some comfort in knowing what lay ahead.

It was not often the winds blew hard enough in Lund for a harbour day, even for my little vessel. But one afternoon, an exceptionally large southeast storm hit the area. Instead of bringing cloud and rain as most winds from that direction did, the day remained fairly sunny and warm and while it was windy, it was not a bad day to be in harbour.

I stopped by a gillnet vessel called the *Ferndale*. It was owned and operated by Don Taylor, from Vancouver. I had met him a few times prior and found him pleasant to talk to, having many stories to tell about his years in the fishing industry. At the time he was a director with the U.F.A.W.U. His son, Dave, would at times travel with him, in his own combination boat. It was not uncommon to see father and son connections in those days, many followed in their fathers' footsteps. Some families on the coast go back many generations in the fishing industry, forging a proud and strong heritage.

On this particular afternoon Don was feeling quite content, having had a good final night gillnetting after a long week on the water. It was mid-afternoon when I caught up with him down at the dock. It was still too rough for me to fish and so I walked over to his boat to say *Hi*. Don asked if I wanted a drink of scotch; it was something I had rarely tried but I agreed to the offer anyway. He had his straight-up, probably the traditional way to enjoy the drink, but not being a true connoisseur, I added 7-Up to mine. We spent the rest of that afternoon talking about everything and anything. It was enjoyable sharing our thoughts. I think it was good for me to have this connection then, with my own father being a long way away in Hamilton; the time with Don that afternoon did in some ways have similarities to a father and son chat. I know he enjoyed himself as well and for many years afterwards, we had a good rapport with each other. The bottle may have run a little low that day but the good time we shared never did.

Time seemed to fly quickly by for some reason and boats were streaming by Lund like geese migrating north. Don, Dave, and many other gillnetters headed for the central coast where net openings would be starting fairly soon. It was at this time that Len and Marian on the *Starlite* and John on the *R.W.* stopped overnight in Lund following the trip from their home port of Ladysmith. It was good to see them and catch up on what had been happening.

Trolling was 'above average' in the lower gulf as well, so they fished near and close to Ladysmith Harbour. This made good sense; it was a bonus to be home every night. I told John about the changes I had made to my boat, pointing out the small ice box and the new radio phone for communication. "What! No oil stove?" he said. "No" was my reply; I still did not have enough extra finances for that. I did have the Coleman stove for cooking on deck and had purchased an extra blanket for the cooler nights up north; that would be the extent of it for now. We shared some time together that evening, but the next morning John and Len left for Port Hardy. I was not going to be far behind.

Chris and I had decided we were leaving on June 15th when the tides would be small, making passage through the narrows more favourable. The day arrived soon enough; after studying the tide book at length we decided to leave late the next morning to catch slack water at Gillard Pass and tie up in Shoal Bay for the first night. Before leaving Lund I finished paying off my bills; what a difference compared to last year, it sure felt good and I even had my own money to go north with.

The next day after saying our goodbyes, Chris and I untied our vessels from the dock. It was nice to now have a radio phone and we picked a quiet channel to communicate on. Being able to talk back and forth would help to break the monotony. Seven hours at the wheel sitting directly above my small but loud diesel engine made for a long and taxing day. We hit slack tide at Gillard Pass as planned and a few hours later we landed in picturesque Shoal Bay. There were several other fish boats already tied up and waiting to leave at the right time the next day. We spent a quiet night there then left with everybody else the following morning. We passed through Green Point Rapids, then Wellbore Channel and entered into Sunderland Channel at the base of Johnstone Strait. I had decided to take the same route as the year before so we turned right at the Broken Group. This was the more sheltered way and like last year I felt it was safer than the open waters of the straits. We tied to the small government dock at Minstrel Island and decided to spend the night. At the time the dock there accommodated vessels like ours who were only passing through, but it also served some of the local logging and tug operations in the area. There was a large building overlooking the wharf area that housed a small pub, store, and post office, and some rooms for the night if needed. A few local fish boats called this place their home year round and Jim on the *Rainbow Falls* was one of the ones I remember. He would often troll or gillnet in the area as he was well set up to do both. A very friendly fellow, whether he knew you or not, Jim liked to exchange stories with anyone and all who passed through, so each of us took our turn telling a few.

We left early the next day with a sky that was grey, overcast and so typical of the west coast climate at this latitude. There was no wind to speak of as we passed through Black Fish Sound then Sointula, eventually arriving in Port Hardy late that afternoon. The harbour was full of boats. There were some trollers, but mainly it was the net fleet tied up waiting for the next two-to-four day opening later in the week. We moored side-by-side, further in at the government wharf and, after shutting down our engines, decided to walk up town. It was good to stretch after sitting so long in our boats and to also enjoy a home cooked meal at Mae's.

Pleasant as it was to be on land, I couldn't wait to get back to my favourite spot at the Deserter Group. The next morning, after we topped up our fuel tanks, I took on a little ice in my new box; this was something new to me. Chris and I then headed our boats over to what we hoped would be the hot spot; even though it wasn't exactly the best time of day. The morning bite would be over, but at least we could get our gear wet and become somewhat comfortable with the tack. Being Chris' first time there he would have an opportunity, like I had the year before, to get familiar with the new surroundings. As we approached the shoreline, I noticed there were no other boats and told Chris over the radio phone I'd be making a wide swing into the edge. Once that was done I put out the gear and slowly moved up the tack. Chris followed close behind me so I could help him get used to the rocks and pinnacles that made up this particular stretch of water.

Intently I watched the sounder, looking for signs of feed, but saw little. Things did not look too promising, but often in the afternoon here, the feed would disappear into deeper water and not show along the edge; the morning would give us the true picture. After three unproductive tacks up and down, we picked up our gear and motored into the narrow channel that led to the anchorage. The now familiar log float from last year was still there, thankfully, and we tied up to it. I could see Chris was taking it all in, this great little part of the coast, so much like myself the year before. Standing in the stern of our boats, we talked, enjoying the quiet serenity of this special place. We tied up a little more gear in readiness for morning and compared what we were going to use; we of course each had our favourite lures.

My stomach was telling me it was nearing dinner time. I fired up the two-burner Coleman stove on the back deck, brought out my always handy cast iron frying pan and made ready to prepare dinner. There was not a lot of choice in my kitchen, it was either fried or boiled. For sure it was not going to be fish that night but who could ever turn down a steak dinner? I even got fancy, adding mushrooms and onions. On the second burner I boiled water for potatoes then opened a can of corn. Though unheated, it would round out the feast; this was going to be dinner fit for a king. Chris had a creation of some kind going on in his boat; as I recall, it was pretty similar to my own. After eating and cleaning up the dishes we talked about a few more things, then shortly after I headed down below and into my tiny bunk. Neither of us had made any money for several days now, but I slowly drifted off to sleep hoping that would change in the morning.

One Big Fish

There was no wind the next morning, only a heavy mist in the air that greeted us as we idled out of the tiny anchorage. The water was a murky green colour and after my gear was in place I was able to concentrate on working my way onto the tack. I made my first turn in at the point where I noticed there was a small ball of feed on the surface. Seeing this was a good sign, as was the fact that we were the only two boats on site. Chris cut in behind me and my first pass yielded nothing. But when turning at the far end I saw Chris land a nice fish. *Where there is one, there should be more*, I thought and then my inside deep line started to bang away. It yielded a fourteen pound salmon. The next couple of hours went by quickly as there was always enough action to keep me busy. It was a constant effort to keep the gear clear of cod and other small fish that were also feeding. True to my past experiences here, early morning on this tack, especially around slack tide, seemed to create a feeding frenzy and that was when things might start to happen. It was now getting close to that time and sure enough, like clockwork, the bite began. I quickly landed another half dozen spring salmon with the biggest being a twenty-five pound beauty. Chris indicated that he had about the same, or one more than me, as usual; the standing jab between us.

The sun had broken clear from the mist just before noon and the air warmed up considerably, so I took off my grey Stanfield pullover. My fish were cleaned and put away in my small ice box and I quickly made a sandwich for lunch. I sat in my stern daydreaming about the moments that had just passed and then I made a large, slow turn in the deep water that was directly in front of the anchorage. I headed back down the tack, staying slightly off the edge and hoping to grab another fish or two. Suddenly as the boat was straightening out my port deep line started to hang way back. *Great,* I thought, *It must be either a small log or kelp that has got caught in the trolling wire and then slid down the line to the lead.* The spring on the poll was stretched straight out and it stayed there. *Funny though,* I thought to myself, *All morning I haven't seen any debris floating on the surface.*

I engaged the clutch on the gurdie drive and started to bring the line in. The line started to slip a little under the weight. In came the first two pieces of gear and as I looked down the line my cannon ball came into view. There was nothing wrapped around it, yet it still hung back from the stern by roughly three feet. I reached down with my gaff and snagged the snap and perlon, the line was very heavy in my hand. I looked back to see what was on the gear and slowly it rose to the surface. At first glance it appeared to be comparable in size to a four by eight sheet of plywood. I could see a dark brown back, mottled by black and white markings throughout. It was huge. I slowly pulled the fish towards the boat, hand over hand and it gradually moved closer. There were two eyes on the top of the head that looked up at me. It did not fight at all but instead seemed rather docile. Now that it was within a few feet of me and fully in view, I realized then that I had caught my first halibut.

I had seen this type of fish being delivered at the plant in Port Hardy, and that was my only means of identifying it. *This* halibut, however, seemed a lot larger than any of the ones I had seen there. It was now up beside my boat. The fish opened its large mouth and shook its head up and down. My arm was strongly jerked back and forth but I held on to the line. I turned and grabbed my gaff and pondered the situation. It would be a timing thing here. I would have to bring it close enough to the boat with my one arm, then slide the gaff into its mouth and bring it aboard. Simple.

The fish was extremely heavy yet I somehow managed to pull it close enough to me with my left hand to be able to slide the gaff into its mouth. At this point it came to life and shook its head violently. Pulling with my right arm I barely managed to get its head out of the water and then the fish shook free from the gaff. The line went slack for a second as the halibut floated back from the moving boat. Once again the line went tight and the cannon ball swayed back under the strain, but amazingly the fish stayed on. I thought for sure the hook would straighten out, or the line would break under the sheer weight but they did not. By now I had tried to angle the boat out into deep water so I could concentrate on the task of landing this fish. However, the extra drag on one side of the *Antique* definitely slowed the boat down and wanted to lead me in the direction of the shore. I had to keep the rudder hard over to counteract all of this. Chris had noticed my change of direction, and later on told me he'd thought something had gone wrong.

Again I started the process of pulling the line in, hand over hand with the gaff still firmly in my grip. When he was in reach I slid the hook into his gaping mouth. I quickly let go of the line and, grasping the gaff with both hands this time, I attempted to bring the fish aboard. Once again it came to life and started to shake its head and body. I stubbornly hung on and, bracing my right foot against the side of the boat, pulled with all my might. Alarmingly, I could see the bulwarks on the *Antique* move slightly under the strain and force of it all. I was twenty four years old at the time, in my prime, and a solid 200 pounds, yet it was all I could do to get that halibut's head out of the water. Something had to give. Ever so slowly the large head of the fish started up the side of my boat, but that was as far as it got. With one final shake of its mighty body the gaff flew from my hands and into the ocean. The fish took a short run and I sort of ducked in self-defence, then the line went slack. The halibut shot back down to the depths from where it came and I was left standing there, kind of mesmerized by the whole experience. I then pulled in the piece of gear it was on, a number 404, six-inch plug and a straightened out hook. Thinking about it later I had to wonder, really, what was I trying to do? I had no idea how heavy this fish was, and where would I have put him anyway? The *Antique* was way too small to carry anything of that size. I picked up my gear and when done, managed to retrieve my gaff that was floating on the surface nearby.

Once back in port I told my story to John and a few others. They all seemed to have their own tales and stories of halibut, especially in reference to the strength of these fish. Basically, it was probably best I left him in the water as he might have torn my little boat apart. When it came to large halibut, what most people would do in smaller boats like mine was to shove a shark hook into its mouth that was tied to 5/16 polyline. Dragging the fish through the water behind the boat would eventually drown it. You'd deliver the fish this way to the plant where it could be winched up from the water and weighed. At that time we could all keep halibut under our A or B licence so that particular fish would have been worth a lot of money. But it was all hindsight now. How big was he? I'll never know. But I did learn that the "he" was probably a "she" as the females are the largest of the species. Based on both the dimensions that I described to people and later seeing some of a similar size delivered, my rough guess was probably between three hundred and four hundred pounds. However, the halibut on this coast have been known to grow twice that size. Even though she got away, that was one fish I never forgot.

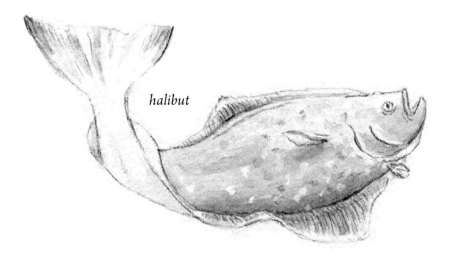

halibut

Fishing improved somewhat over the next few weeks as more fish moved into the area. I stayed pretty much at the Deserter Group, as did Chris. Funny how he grew to like this spot so much and he also became a homesteader. My small ice box served its purpose well, allowing me that extra night stay-over, and I would deliver every second day.

My friends stuck to their favourite spots as well; we would see each other during deliveries. John usually alternated between Masterman and Duval Point, close to Port Hardy. Len and Marian, as always, fished their little spot at the Jeanette Islands, where they had the place to themselves. They'd fish in the strong tides that were common there yet they always managed to make a season of it. Occasionally I would have a quick look and check out the Gordon Group on the way back to the Deserters, but as usual I never seemed to do very much there. I just didn't have confidence in the place and most likely that had something to do with it.

Over the next few days things really slowed down. Tides were building and I entertained the idea of moving on to some new ground. This season, however, was an "on" year for Fraser River pinks, the smallest of the five salmon species. The name referred basically to the colour of their flesh, that being a light pink. They were now beginning to trickle in from the outside waters. A small fleet of boats working Christy Pass about one hour west of the Deserters were starting to catch a few. The trouble was there was little money in pink fishing; at best you were paid twenty-five to thirty cents a pound. Basically you'd have to catch approximately forty-five pink salmon at four to five pounds each to equal the value of one twenty-five pound spring salmon. Pink, or humpback salmon as they were also referred to, were easy to catch. They are voracious eaters and bite on just about everything. To catch big numbers, you'd simply put more gear in the water. Flashers with a small pink hoochie behind worked the best as they resembled their favourite food, shrimp. It was not uncommon, however, to catch them on spoons or plugs.

After delivering to the cannery, I picked up some extra gear at the Port Hardy fuel dock then started tying up flashers in order to get ready for my first run of pink salmon. I used red Hot Spot flashers with a twenty-seven inch tail, much shorter than the forty-two inch set-up for spring salmon. I'd put a flasher on every mark on the main line so I needed heavier cannon balls to be able to get all that gear down to its proper depth. Every two years was the cycle for this Fraser River run of fish which could get as big as eight pounds. They were probably the largest in average size of any other particular pink run on the coast and there was a good spawn in the river on the last cycle. The return was expected to be above average.

A couple of days later I relocated to Christy Pass and decided to give 'pink' fishing a go. There's a lighthouse at Scarlet Point marking the outside entranceway to the passage. As fish moved down from above, it became a good spot for us "inside boats" to catch them. There was a small group of maybe ten boats that steadily worked the tack back and forth. It was a somewhat sheltered place and well-suited for my small boat. I could fish the beach or move out to deeper water, as hugging an edge was not as critical when catching these fish. They often arrived in big schools and hence covered a larger area.

Some of these fish came from the local streams and were

smaller, at maybe three to four pounds. Hardy Bay had a pink run and so did Knights Inlet. These fish would usually arrive first as their spawning cycle was different than the Fraser run, moving up stream earlier in late August; the Fraser run was more toward September/October.

When fishing pink salmon you were always very busy, especially being by yourself. The work was constant, either pulling them aboard or cleaning them. There were packers anchored close by in the pass at a small bay, just behind Scarlet Point. For us day boats these packers were a viable and necessary option. We did not have to clean the fish if we had a large volume because they also would buy in the round. Selling that way, however, meant less money per pound, you were paid a little more to dress them. Usually the seine and gillnet boats sold in the round as they could often deliver extremely large numbers.

I remember one foggier morning a group of us were trolling just outside the pass. The day had started off with a light fog but as the morning progressed it thickened. I stayed close to the beach and in sight of land; yet inside the pass I could see it was clear. I decided not fight both Mother Nature and the other boats and picked up my gear. I idled the *Antique* into the pass and decided I'd try to catch a spring salmon. I had never trolled for these salmon here as it was not known to be a hot spot. *But let's give it a try, anyway*, I thought. I stowed the pink gear away in a small cardboard box and set up the boat for spring salmon. My first tack up the shoreline produced a thirty-five pound fish and a smile on my face. This was a great start, and I had the whole place to myself. At the end of the pass I turned and headed toward the other shoreline. Straightening out I headed up the beach towards a place called God's Pocket. Another fish started to yard on my deep line and it looked big, as the spring stretched in and out to its maximum. When that salmon neared the surface it jumped clear out of the water, trying to shake the hook. It was a wild fish. Back and forth he darted but finally I had him up alongside the stern of the boat and, gaffing him, I lifted the prize into my checkers. He was a beauty. This one was almost as big as the first. I quickly checked the sounder and angled out as the bottom had started to come up. *Better not go this far up around next time,* I thought and filed the information in my memory bank. From here I continued back over to the opposite shore and repeated this kind of large circular tack all over again. There was nothing the second time around but by noon I had landed two more nice fish. Four good size spring salmon sure brightened up the day. Some of the boats fishing pinks outside of me had two hundred for the day but I took great pride in knowing that my four spring salmon were worth the same amount of money and that they had been a whole lot more fun to catch.

I tried the same thing again next morning but had no luck, not even a bite. Most spring salmon here were travelling through and didn't stick around for long. Meanwhile Chris was still fishing at the Deserter Group and I contacted him by radio phone but learned from him that it remained slow there as well. I decided to stay at the pass and put the pink gear back out as the fog had dissipated somewhat. During my time there I saw some familiar faces but also met some new people along the way. I remember meeting Al Richards and his brother; they based out of Hardwick Island and had a boat at the time called the *Sea Song*. At night I'd tie up to other vessels or raft to one of four can buoys in God's Pocket; anchoring for me was still not the preferred option.

"Stormin'" Norman and Dan, who pretty much travelled and fished together, passed by on their way to sell in Port Hardy. The weather outside was not good that day but the fish were really starting to show up. I was content for the time being to wait it out at Christy Pass. By now, however, I had a growing interest and often wondered about these waters. I'd hear stories about the open Pacific and the ground swells that came with it but also felt drawn to the possibility of better fishing; all this helped to fuel my curiosity.

So one day in early August, I felt it was time to give "outside fishing" a try in the *Antique*. I awoke that morning to an overcast sky with a light drizzle but very little wind. If anything, there was a southeast breeze, making for ideal conditions in which to attempt my first day offshore; I'd be somewhat in the lee of Vancouver Island, with a wind coming from that direction. Pine Island and the lighthouse there marked one of the gateways to the open Pacific but I decided to follow a small group of boats heading for Bates Passage. This led to Shadwell Pass and once through this short stretch of water I would be entering the open waters. I could see a light groundswell ahead of me here, just enough for me to get the feel of it. I was a little nervous to say the least but once the gear was in the water it helped to settle the boat down.

The tide was ebbing so I'd get a good push out in the morning. I stayed a little outside of everyone else and away from the shallow sandy edge known as the drop-off. Fish would often lie up against this bank, moving in and out with the tide. As I idled further out, the slight groundswell started to increase a little. With the up and down motion the open ocean offered, I had to be extremely aware of my surroundings. Large floating kelp beds and logs could suddenly appear from nowhere. These floating islands were quite large and tangling with one would not have been good as they could probably strip your lines of gear.

The sea was dotted with birds of all types, some I had never seen before. They were feeding on the rich abundance of food in the area and the place was alive. There were puffins with their large orange bills. They would disappear under water for minutes at a time and then reappear on the surface usually with a small fish in their bill. My hands gripped the wheel as my boat rode up a larger than normal swell. Then I seemed to disappear as I slid back down the other side. I kept the little bow pointed directly into the sea. This rise and fall was certainly a different experience than anything I had been used to. When I rode to the top of a wave I could look west, and as far as I could see there was open water, except for a line of about thirty or forty boats all going in the same direction. Then when I slid down into the trough they would disappear from sight.

I jumped into the stern after checking that the water ahead was clear and I pulled up my deep line, taking about five pink salmon off the line. There were definitely fish here. The line on the other side had just as many pinks with a couple of Coho thrown into the mix. All in all, twenty-five fish came off the gear on that first go around. Again I had a quick look ahead of me before starting the process of cleaning my catch. The larger boats of course all had deckhands for this, but I was happy being a one man band; there really wasn't room for anyone else.

Most of the morning went smoothly and by noon I found myself a fair way off shore. A slight breeze from the southwest had started to pick up and the ocean swells had grown even larger. Nervously, I turned the boat around and took the swells directly on my stern. My little boat rode the waves not too badly when facing them head on but stern quarter was not so much fun.

The wind freshened a little more as it often did before a tide change, and with the last of the ebb tide moving against the incoming swells, some of the waves grew quite a bit larger than normal. Up the *Antique* went then back down she came, as the bottom, at times, seemed to fall away from under me. I was really starting to not like this. The boats in the distance seemed to grow even smaller in the surrounding waters as the sea continued to build. I must have appeared almost non-existent to the others being probably the smallest boat out there. Looking at the *Antique* from afar would have been like seeing a large floating log with a couple of branches sticking out from it. By 2:00 p.m. the tide was on the flood but I'd had enough. Quickly I pulled in my gear and once it was aboard I opened my motor up, keeping the stern pointed directly into the incoming swells. As I got closer to where I had first started that morning, the waves seemed to dissipate a little.

Eventually, a couple hours later, I slid back into the more sheltered waters of Bates Passage and headed back down to Christie Pass. There were some fish in the checkers to clean so it was not a wasted effort, but still I was not in too big of a hurry to go back there. Fishing the outside was something I wanted to do and I did. However, it was to be the only time I'd ever take the *Antique* out into off-shore waters; yet another vivid memory for me.

The next day I returned to the Deserter Group to try my luck again with spring salmon but it remained spotty as many fish had now passed through, heading for their spawning grounds. I had the odd day that was encouraging, catching maybe half a dozen fish, but then the next, I might only catch two. Time was running out, it was nearing mid-August and I needed to be pursuing guaranteed money. The Fraser River pink run would be more of a sure thing than scratching away for springs here and there.

On the last day fishing the Deserters I delivered what fish I had into Port Hardy. I then heard that John had an accident that very morning and was in the local clinic. He was fishing Masterman Island and had a big spring up behind his boat. Placing his handgun on the cap rail within easy reach, he made ready to take a shot in order to stun the fish. For whatever reason, and whether the boat took a quick list or not is vague, but the gun fell to the floor and went off. The bullet passed through his leg above the kneecap, barely missing the bone. As in any situation like this, it could always have been worse. John was alright but in some pain; his season was basically over. A couple of days later John would travel south to Ladysmith by car, leaving the *R.W.* in Port Hardy. Eventually, after a month of rest, he was able to return to get his boat. Before driving home, we spent some time together and then said our farewells; I would miss him.

Mitchell Bay

As for me, I decided to head south to Malcolm Island; Seafoods had a fish camp located near the bottom end, in a sheltered place called Mitchell Bay. The camp was run by Kathy and Spence Turner, a local couple who lived permanently on the island. As I remember, they also had a fellow named Hank working with them; he would help with the grading and weighing of the fish. Kathy looked after the small store beside the weigh station and Spence ran one of the packers, the *Naomi K,* which transported fish from here to the Port Hardy cannery. At the peak, when the fish were really moving through these waters, another packer, the Mitchell Bay was called into action. It alternated its runs to town with Spence's boat. At this time of year Spence and Kathy were extremely busy; there were many boats in the area and I knew many of the fishermen.

After tying my boat up to a small temporary float, I entered the store. I learned there had been some big scores that particular day, ranging anywhere from one hundred to three hundred fish. Even at the fairly low prices, those numbers made for good money. I purchased a couple of items I'd forgotten and needed, then introduced myself to Kathy at the till. I was immediately impressed by her warm and friendly greeting. Running a camp is a big job, especially at this time of year when the fish are passing through; things can get a little hectic. Kathy and Spence had to adjust to the frantic pace as it had been fairly slow and quiet for them up until now, but they were ready for it. Over the time I spent there, I came to realize that Kathy was a rock in many ways. No matter how busy it got she always had a smile for everyone and at the same time kept everything running smoothly.

The following morning I untied my lines and left with the rest of the fleet. It was overcast with a morning mist, but fortunately no fog, something this area was very susceptible to at this time of year. I rounded Donegal Head and entered the swirling currents of Blackfish Sound. While relativity sheltered from the wind, the tide could run hard here. It was known as a place where fish returning to the south coast would stop, mill about, feed and rest in preparation for their long run down coast through Johnstone Strait. There was usually a pod of killer whales in the area and, with all that food available to them, they often stayed here for quite a while, hence the name Black Fish Sound.

I was ready for action with my gear freshly retied and added a few more flashers to each of my lines. *The more hooks in the water, the more fish*, I reminded myself. Trolling down the west side of the sound towards Double Bay, I dropped my first line into the water and felt the fish already starting to hit the gear. This was fun. Not wanting to wait, I pulled the line immediately back up and took eight pink salmon off ten pieces of gear. I then sent the line back down and put out the other three so that all four were working. This made for forty flashers in all. Using more gear helped to resemble a school of fish feeding on shrimp. This simulated-action would attract fish to your boat and hopefully excite them into biting. If you had a big enough school following, you could pull steadily for several hours. I looked up and saw that all four lines were pulling away. When one fish stopped moving, I would see another hit and the pole springs would stretch back and forth vigorously again. It was best to wait until you thought you had one fish to each hook and then pull up one line at a time. I started in the back lines first because if there was a school behind them, the incoming gear would lead the fish into the flashers on the deep lines. This technique increased the chances that the fish would continue to follow your boat. On my first full go around I pulled thirty-five fish aboard. Not too bad. My small checker box had never been so full before.

The nice thing with this type of fishing was there was always something to do. As I started cleaning my catch I looked up and saw that fish were again climbing on. The bite seemed to be in full force so I decided to concentrate on just pulling fish. This went on for two full hours. When it slowed down I again started cleaning my catch as quickly and thoroughly as I could. I must have been a blur of activity, between checking my bearings, cleaning and washing the fish. I stayed off the edge and ventured into deep water to lessen any worries of gear hang-ups. It was good to have my ice box at this time; it sure made for more space on board and as well, a place to store my finished product. At the present catch rate, though, it would be full fairly soon.

Some of the bigger male fish had started to form a large hump on their back, hence their name humpback salmon. There appeared to be about a five-pound weight average, with some of the bigger fish dressing out at seven pounds. I had trolled against the tide in one direction for most of this time and, having just reached the bottom end of the sound, I made my turn and headed back the other way. Once I had finished cleaning the fish on board, I started to go through the gear again. By this time I guessed I had about 125 fish in the boat with the odd one still biting as I worked my way back up the sound. After I finished cleaning the last of those, my stomach was now aching with hunger. I made a quick couple of non-fish sandwiches, then with renewed energy, I went back through the gear. That produced twenty-five more fish; not bad, but still, it was after a fairly long soak.

I moved back up the tack fairly quickly as the tide was running with me and pointed the boat towards Donegal Head, the bottom end of Malcolm Island. Looking around I could see that there were boats all through the sound, in the middle and as far over as Bold Head on the opposite shoreline. But I was content to stay here, being that it was not nearly as crowded and also there were no hang-ups on this side. In the middle of the sound and closer to the opposite shore there was a sharp pinnacle called Egeria Shoal, a rock that rises up from the deep to sixteen fathoms. It comes at you quickly and can instantly strip your gear off. Most of us had our lines set anywhere from twenty-five to forty fathoms, so hitting this obstacle could be costly. I stayed clear of it, but once in a while, looking in that direction you would see a puff of smoke coming from an exhaust pipe. That usually meant a boat was on top of the rock and was speeding up to try and raise the gear up and over it. On my side of the sound you had to watch the flood tide around Stubbs Island, as the water ran very strong through there. If you got too close in you could basically sit in the same spot for a long time. So I stayed out a little bit and further away when passing by that place.

Fishing slowed down in the afternoon and by 5:30 I called it a day and headed in to deliver my catch. My checkers were full and the ice box as well, with an estimated 175 fish for my efforts. Of course there were plenty that had done the same and the unloading dock in Mitchell Bay was surrounded by boats. I had to wait as it was first come, first served. There were about five boats ahead of me so I tied alongside one that I knew and talked about the day, patiently awaiting our turn. Soon I was next and, in very short order, was unloaded. I tied my boat to another float nearby and after cleaning up, it was off to the store to get my tally. The air was full of talk; fishermen compared notes and the buzz was all about who had caught what and where. I bought a steak from the store and headed back to my boat. It was now time to relax and prepare dinner, tomorrow would come soon enough.

Chris arrived a couple of days later as it had become way too scratchy at the Deserters. It was good to have him in radio range; now we could compare notes and help to keep each other on the "hot spot".

The fishing here remained pretty steady for us right through until the end of the first week in September; then it seemed to drop off drastically. Many boats started to head south while others went north to pursue the later fall Coho runs. By now I had put in close to three pretty good weeks here which certainly helped my total earnings for the year. I calculated approximately how much money I had made to date and started to plan where it would go.

Thoughts of moving a step up to a bigger boat were certainly going through my mind at the time. I really needed a larger vessel that could take me to more remote places on the coast; basically I wanted an outside troller. I had seen enough boats unloading in Port Hardy with full holds from the outside waters to realize what my next step had to be. Some of them were at sea for up to eight days and when delivering, could take up to two hours to unload. There were some good seasons being put in and a lot had to do with the size of the vessel and their increased holding capacities. However, it all came down to money; there was a price to be paid for all of this. After this year the *Antique* had only two more salmon seasons left on it then its B licence expired. I needed an A licence vessel, which meant the salmon privilege was renewable every year and never ran out. It would help to further secure my place in the fishery.

Chris came over for a chat one day after selling his catch; we had a beer and compared notes. As always, we discussed how each of us had done. He had heard the largest catches were made on the Bold Head side of the sound, but we both knew that a fisherman cannot be everywhere at once. Basically we hadn't done too badly for ourselves either and we both felt satisfied. I cooked a nice fresh pink salmon for our dinner that night, so good when right out of the water. They are known as being an oily fish and it certainly made for a very juicy meal.

At about this time, both Chris and I were feeling the urge to head back home to Lund. The idea had been building for a couple of days now and after catching *only* twenty-five pinks for a good part of one morning, we decided it was time to leave. I went in to unload and get the boat ready for the trip south, as did Chris. We first checked the tide book so we could figure out the appropriate time to leave Mitchell Bay. It appeared we would have to get an early start the next morning in order to catch the ideal tides through the rapids. We topped up our fuel tanks, checked everything over and then said our goodbyes to Spence, Kathy and Hank. We thanked them for their warm hospitality and the memorable times we'd had there. I did not know it then but that would be the one and only time I ever fished out of Mitchell Bay. The little camp would close down a few years later, much like so many others of its kind. There were, of course, always packers in the area, but many of the fish buyers seemed to be pushing for more centrally located parts of the coast for deliveries, such as Port Hardy and Vancouver. Basically, the cost of running small floating camps had become too expensive. This was a sad reality; it would soon be a lot harder to run and operate a small day boat such as the *Antique*. Changes were definitely in the air.

Final Trip Home

The morning of our departure Chris and I awoke to what looked to be an ideal day for travelling. The days were becoming cooler as fall was not far off; there was a definite chill in the air and hot coffee first thing was a necessity. Within a half hour our two boats were idling into the calm waters of Black Fish Sound. We glided through Blackney Pass, where the tide swirled somewhat as tons of water from the sound was squeezed through this narrow passage. We had the last of the flood tide with us, pushing our boats out the other side and then into the open waters of Johnstone Straits. This was the preferred route at the time because the weather was with us; from here, Lund was only about 12 hours away.

The Strait is a major travelling lane for boats of all kinds on the coast. There were tugs and barges, large cruise vessels and many fish boats that morning, all making for a busy stretch of water. Sitting at the wheel I daydreamed about having been away from my home port for so long and tingled with the anticipation of arriving there. We had so many stories to share. Such thoughts were in my mind as we made our way south towards Lund, and I'm sure Chris was feeling the same.

Suddenly, as we neared the Broken Islands, Chris's voice came through on the radio phone. He said he was having engine problems; his motor was running sporadically and missing. While this could be caused by several things, most likely it indicated water in the fuel. I stood by while he quickly drained and changed the filter. Sure enough there was water there; not a good thing. He soon had his boat underway but it still continued to act up. After an hour of this we were nearing Port Neville and getting closer to Sunderland Channel. It was here that his engine quit altogether so I decided we should tie up and keep moving so as not to miss the tides at the narrows. There was a lot less vessel traffic here as most of the other boats went the Seymour Narrows route, so rafting together was not a bad option. Less traffic meant more space and also fewer swells from passing boats. All we had for protection then between our vessels were four black rubber tires, a common form of bumper in those days.

All of a sudden my motor started to miss and then quit running altogether. *Great, now what?* In a diesel engine, when this happens, it can be air or water in the fuel system and I immediately checked all four injectors. The third one had a light sheen of fuel around its base. Putting my wrench around it I discovered that it was a tiny bit loose. I turned the motor over for a couple of seconds to allow any air to leave the system then I tightened the injector back down and sure enough the motor came to life. What a relief! I had a close look at everything before engaging the clutch. With my power once again restored we were both back underway, having lost only about fifteen minutes of running time. Mechanics had never been my strong suit but when you're dealing with a boat, learning some of the basics and keeping components running properly is a necessity. *Let's hope this is the last of it,* I thought to myself.

We travelled this way for the next while, with the two boats running off only my engine, and everything seemed to be back to normal. My biggest concern was that we had lost some ground and time. I calculated we had to arrive at Wellbore Chanel three hours ahead of the change to flood tide. That would give us slack water through Gillard Pass, which was by far the worst stretch to travel through. Soon enough we entered Wellbore Chanel and immediately felt the surge of the ebb tide against us. It was slow going as the water swirled around us and our boats gently rolled back against each other. The two boats and the two skippers were not always on the same page. Being not very visible to each other at times, Chris would be angling one way while I was going another. It was an impossible situation but what could we do? Meanwhile, Chris periodically tried to restart his engine but it would only run for a short moment then quit. His battery was now running low and at this point he had to give up on it altogether.

Once we were through Wellbore Channel we moved into a more open stretch of water. The next obstacle ahead was Green Point Rapids.

I was constantly looking at the clock and the shoreline to gauge our speed as time was now of the essence. We arrived at Green Point at slack water so all was smooth travelling through there and shortly after we got the much needed push from the flood tide. It was obvious by now we were going to be late for Gillard Pass, but after a short discussion we both decided to go for it. The tides were not overly large, so how bad could it be? We could have tied up at Shoal Bay but that would mean waiting for the next favourable tide the following morning. The strong urge to get home was tugging at both of us. Passing slowly by Shoal Bay I noticed quite a few boats tied up to the floats; obviously they were not in such a hurry to go anywhere. Once past there our decision to press on became more of a reality; we were soon reaching the point of no turning back.

I know we both had doubts and unspoken concerns with this decision. Neither of us said anything. Instead, we added a few lines to fortify our flotilla. We made sure our bumpers were secured in the right place, thereby doing our best to protect the two boats. We then had a quick discussion on just where we should best navigate this stretch of water; I wanted to enter Devil's Hole closer to the shoreline on the right side. We were fast approaching this spot and, sure enough, time wise it looked like we were a solid two hours after slack. There was a tension in the air and my hands were sweating. My stomach felt uneasy and I was far more nervous than in any of my previous passes through here. It was almost like the calm before the storm; we were entering the unknown.

Suddenly we were in it and rapidly gained speed. A series of small whirlpools, back-eddies and boiling water churned ahead of us as the boats began to tug at each other. Through our wheelhouse windows I pointed to Chris to go hard over to starboard and I did the same to avoid Devil's Hole. There was only evidence of a small whirlpool here and we quickly sped by it. But the current still felt strong regardless. The passage now opens up a little but only for a short stretch before it narrows back down at the entrance to Gillard Pass. I could see the light on the point that marked the far end. *Not much further to go now*, I thought to myself. My hands were tightly gripped around the small steering wheel and I understood now what the term "white knuckles" meant. The water was boiling up around the shoreline as we entered the passage, with the tide by now running at around four to five knots. We quickly shot through the gut and sped past the flashing light. *That didn't seem to be too bad*, I thought. However, when I looked ahead, a sudden grip of fear went through my body. A huge whirl pool that looked to be about fifty feet in diameter was in our path. I looked at Chris and he looked at me and I again pointed to the right. Starboard was the direction we had to go anyway but more importantly I wanted to avoid the middle of the vortex that loomed in front of us. A second seemed an eternity. In no time at all we were on its front edge and while our boats were headed in the right direction our control lasted but only a second as the current dictated to us where *it* wanted us to go. We straightened out slightly and the boats started to bang and crash against each other as our tie up lines held us both captive. Looking out the side of my window I could see a hole in the water, kind of like a funnel, that marked the centre of the whirlpool. Hitting the backside, we did a complete 180 degree spin in seconds and now were now facing the far shore. Out back through the wheel house door I could see water all over my deck as the ocean spray shot up between our boats. The line joining our poles went slack then taut and I could see my bull works moving in and out under the strain of it. I wanted to cut the line with a knife at that point and free the two boats from each other's grip before we tore our poles down. This would have given us a little more freedom to move, and we would still have our bow and stern lines connecting us. But there was no time for that. The surging water started to slightly draw us in then suddenly spun us around and spat us out as if we were nothing but two pieces of driftwood. We continued sideways down the channel, facing the far shore, and I fought hard at the wheel to try and get our bows pointed in the right direction. Ever so slowly my boat responded and finally, the current subsided; we were free of its grip. Then, rounding a small point of land, the Stuart Island Lodge came into view. I directed our two boats towards the small tie-up float.

Both Chris and I were visibly shaken as we stepped out onto the dock to tie up. At this point I'd totally had enough for one day. In our urgency to get home we'd put ourselves unnecessarily in and through a truly dangerous situation. So many things could have potentially gone wrong here, but fortunately they didn't. Looking back now, we were lucky to have got away with it. I do believe someone was watching over us that day.

Respect the ocean. Those three simple words that my friend Henry had said to me when I first started fishing not so long ago now jumped to mind. In this case, I had not respected her and it could have been a costly lesson. There is a common saying I have heard over the years and that is "A boat will usually take more than you." Of course this has to be within reason and you have to know the limits of your vessel. On this particular day, the *Antique* took way more than she deserved, but she somehow managed to get us both through it.

After collecting our thoughts, we eventually wandered up the ramp to the small lounge/restaurant in the main lodge; I do remember how good it felt to once again be on solid ground. After having a bite to eat we went back to our boats and closely checked everything over; all seemed to be fine. However, by now I was both tired and drained. It seemed, for the first time that day, we were not in a big hurry to go somewhere. I went down to my bunk to rest and quickly drifted off into a deep sleep.

In the morning we again started out and travelled with a group of boats, probably those who had spent a quiet night in Shoal Bay. After an uneventful four hour run we idled into Lund harbour, still rafted together, and tied up to the government dock. The tiny vessels that had taken us away months before had now delivered us safely home.

Epilogue

I was in the 25ᵗʰ year of my life and the winds of change were certainly swirling around me. I had fished the *Antique* for two seasons and with only two more years left on the B licence I felt it was time to make a change. My ambitions and confidence had, over that time, grown. I was now ready for a larger vessel with an A licence. The cramped quarters, too, I guess, had taken their toll and I longed for a little more space and a few of the luxuries that would come with it. For sure, the oil stove for heat and cooking was a must. A sink would be a plus and better anchor gear with a winch could also be put on the wish list. A more modern sounder and up-to-date radio phones for communication would be a bonus and let's not forget, radar.

I had some finances saved after a fairly successful 1976 season and felt that things were in place for me to make the step up. The next boat would be expensive, however, the opportunity to catch more fish also meant the opportunity to make more money. It would be worth the risk. I suppose in some ways I had outgrown the little boat.

My days in Lund were also coming to an end as I made plans to move to Port Hardy that fall. There were other factors that led to the changes in my life and it was time to move on. When I tied the *Antique* to the Lund dock the day of my return, I didn't realize it then, but it would be for the final time. I ran an ad in *The Vancouver Sun* and placed a For Sale sign in her window. Shortly thereafter I headed back to Port Hardy where I had already found a job in the woods logging. Art, Millie and

Henry agreed to keep an eye on the *Antique* for me and with that looked after I said farewell to everyone.

In December of that year I had a buyer for the boat. I travelled by bus from Port Hardy to Courtenay then took a ferry to Powell River, where Chris picked me up by car. The buyer was from Courtenay, and we decided that for the sake of convenience, the exchange would take place in the middle of the Gulf of Georgia outside of a place called Grants Reef, about half way between Courtenay and Lund. It probably was not the most common way to finalize and complete a transaction, but that is how we did it.

On the designated day and time I headed the *Antique* across the gulf. Chris idled beside me in his speedboat; he would be my return ride to Lund. The waters were flat calm but it was slow going; there were barnacles and grass all over the bottom of the *Antique*'s hull from sitting idle for so long. The buyer was there already, waiting for us when we slowly drifted up beside their small boat. He would return to his home port in the *Antique*. We had a short discussion about everything boat related and then, after shaking hands, we exchanged the necessary paperwork. I climbed into Chris' waiting boat and took a seat up front, beside him. He pointed the bow in the opposite direction and opened up the throttle. I glanced back only once; it was all I could do. With my eyes straight ahead, we motored quietly back to Lund; I never looked back.

There is another saying I've heard, and that is, "A boat can grow on you". So true. Although it was a somber day for me, with the money from the sale, I would have enough to move forward. And that I did. In late January, after a fair bit of looking, I eventually bought another boat. I stepped up to a 36 foot A licence troller called the *Willmar II*; my next dream had become a reality.

The *Antique* had served me well and had taken me to the next stage of my fishing career: this story is definitely a testament to that. Without knowing it then, she was at the forefront of what eventually led to thirty *proud* years in the west coast fishing industry.

This story is also a tribute to so many of the people I met along the way and, of course, to that small community located at the end of a road. Lund, in many ways, was a "start" for me.

About ten years ago I was at a prawn fishing meeting in Campbell River and ran into the fellow who had bought the *Antique*. It had been a long time since that day. Recognizing me, he came over and we had a lengthy conversation over lunch. I learned then that he trolled salmon with the boat for its final two years in the Gulf of Georgia and when the licence expired he used the *Antique* to fish for cod. Sadly, one day, for whatever reason he didn't say, she succumbed to the elements and sank somewhere in the deep waters off Courtenay.

Like so many of the boats from her day that had met with the same fate, this was a sad ending. I have never forgotten the *Antique* and the special moments and times we shared then. When looking back now, I can honestly say that in so many ways, those first two seasons were my "golden years" of fishing.

Acknowledgments

A big thank you to my family for their support over the many years it took to write this story. To Michaela and Justin, for always having such a positive response whenever I would say, "What do you think of this?" after having read a new or corrected segment to you. Your thoughts have always meant a lot and certainly helped inspire me to carry on.

And to my wife, Joan, for everything you did to help bring this book to completion. I will never forget that special Christmas gift, awhile back now, when you took all of my hand-printed words and scribblings, complete with arrows and cross-outs, then managed to figure it all out and present to me the very first typed version. That was no easy task. But it should have come as no surprise; it is so like everything you have ever done. As a Mother and Partner, you have simply been *the best*.

Always.